HISTORY

OF THE

WAR IN SOUTH AFRICA

1899–1902

COMPILED BY DIRECTION OF
HIS MAJESTY'S GOVERNMENT

BY

MAJOR-GENERAL SIR FREDERICK MAURICE, K.C.B.

WITH A STAFF OF OFFICERS

MAPS • VOLUME III

The Naval & Military Press Ltd

Published by
The Naval & Military Press Ltd
5 Riverside, Brambleside, Bellbrook
Industrial Estate, Uckfield, East Sussex,
TN22 1QQ England
Tel: +44 (0) 1825 749494
Fax: +44 (0) 1825 765701
www.naval-military-press.com

In reprinting in facsimile from the original, any imperfections are inevitably reproduced and the quality may fall short of modern type and cartographic standards.

LIST OF MAPS AND FREEHAND SKETCHES.
VOL. III.

MAPS.

No. 38.	NORTH OF THE ORANGE FREE STATE AND PART OF THE TRANSVAAL.
No. 39.	THE PASSAGE OF THE ZAND RIVER. May 10th, 1900. *Situation about 9.45 a.m.*
No. 40.	THE PASSAGE OF THE VAAL RIVER. May 24th to 27th, 1900.
No. 41.	THE ACTION AT DOORN KOP. May 29th, 1900. *Situation about 4 p.m.*
No. 42.	THE ACTION AT SIX MILE SPRUIT. June 4th, 1900. *Situation about 3 p.m.*
No. 43	NORTH WEST OF CAPE COLONY.
No. 44.	DIAMOND HILL. June 11th, 1900. *Situation about 3 p.m.*
No. 44.(A).	DIAMOND HILL. *Situation on June 12th, 1900.*
No. 45.	NORTHERN NATAL AND PART OF THE TRANSVAAL. May 8th to July 6th, 1900. *Illustrating Sir R. Buller's advance from Ladysmith into the Transvaal.*
No. 46.	LAING'S NEK AND BOTHA'S PASS. June 8th, 1900.
No. 47.	ALLEMAN'S NEK. June 11th, 1900. *Situation about 3.30 p.m.*
No. 48.	EASTERN TRANSVAAL. August 6th to 10th, 1900. *Showing the first stage of the combined advance on Komati Poort.*
No. 49.	BELFAST TO KOMATI POORT. September 3rd to 24th, 1900. *Showing the second stage of the combined advance on Komati Poort.*
No. 50.	THE ATTACK ON BERGENDAL FARM. August 25th, 1900. *Situation prior to the final assault.*
No. 51.	ENVIRONS OF MAFEKING.
No. 52.	DEFENCE OF MAFEKING. October, 1899, to May, 1900. *Showing all defence works constructed throughout the siege.*
No. 53.	BRANDWATER BASIN AND ADJOINING COUNTRY.
No. 54.	NORTH CAPE COLONY AND PART OF THE ORANGE FREE STATE.
No. 55.	INDEX MAP TO VOLUME III.

FREEHAND SKETCHES.

VIEW OF MAFEKING FROM THE SOUTH.
VIEW FROM MAFEKING TO THE SOUTH.
VIEW EAST-SOUTH-EAST FROM LAING'S NEK.
ALLEMAN'S NEK AS SEEN FROM THE SOUTH-WEST.
ZILIKAT'S NEK FROM THE SOUTH.
BRANDWATER BASIN BETWEEN FICKSBURG AND FOURIESBURG.
RETIEF'S NEK.
COUNTRY BETWEEN NAAUWPOORT NEK AND GOLDEN GATE.
VIEW OF THE WITTE BERGEN.
THE BRANDWATER BASIN ABOUT SLAAP KRANZ.
COUNTRY NEAR KOMATI POORT.

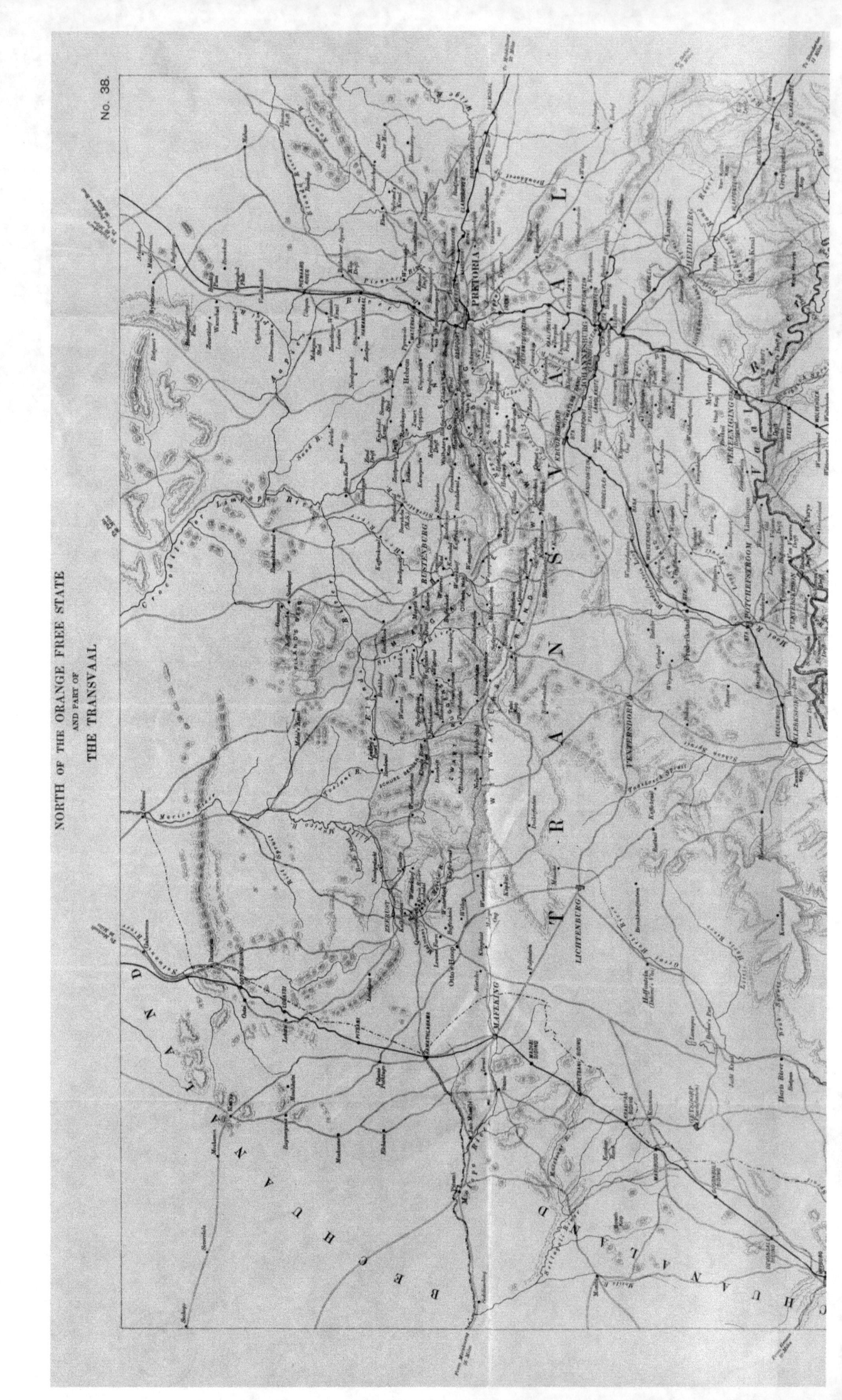

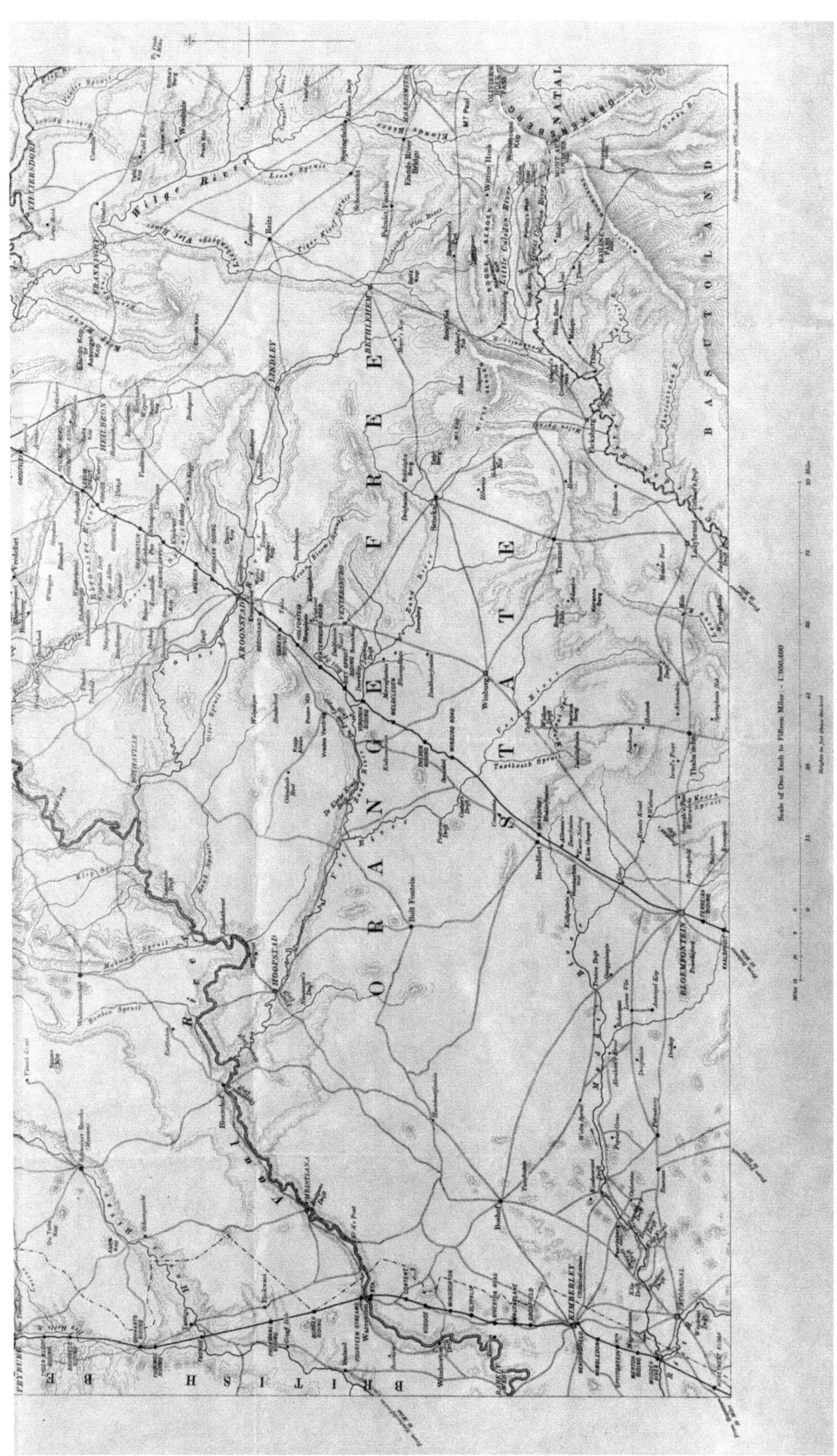

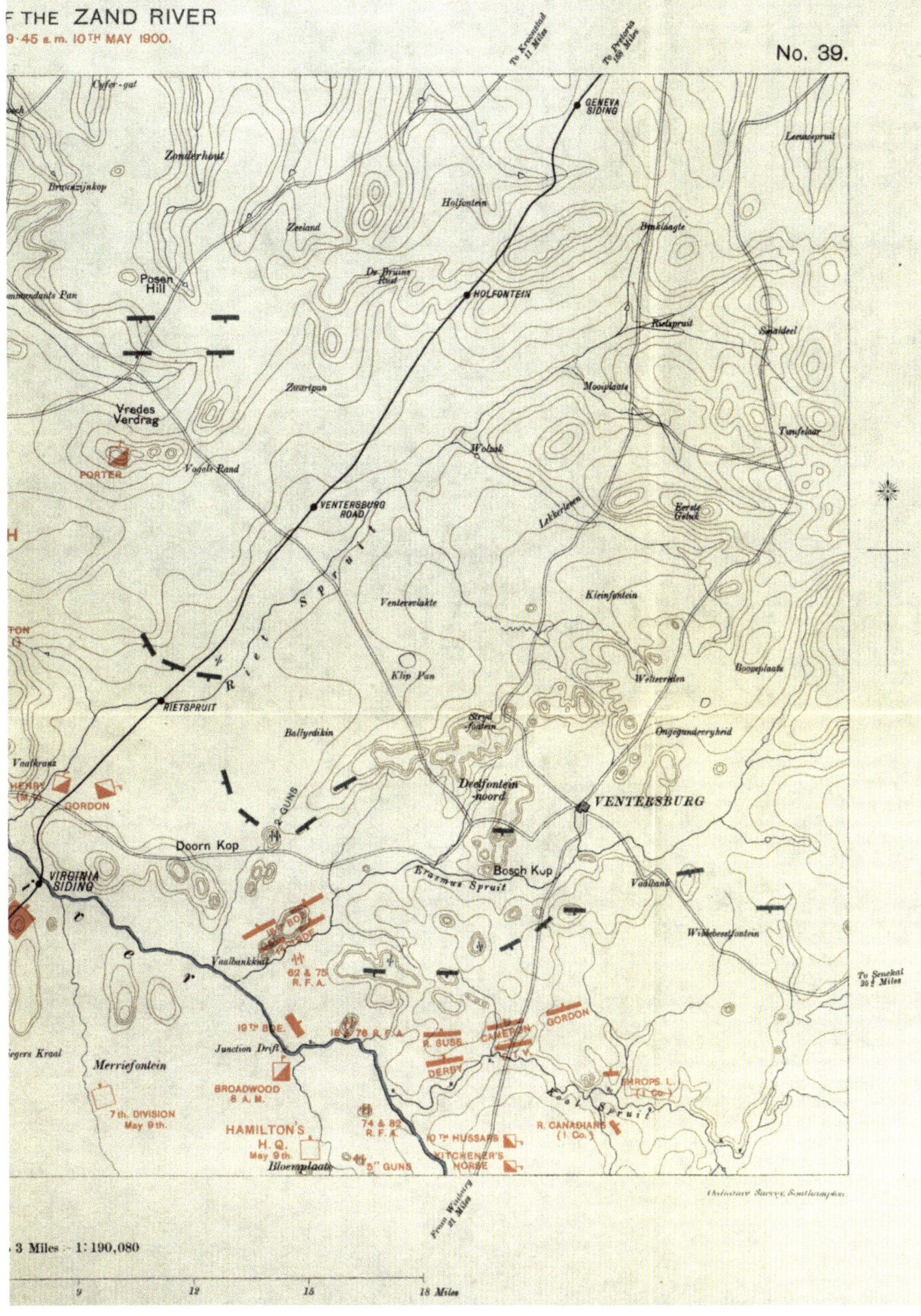

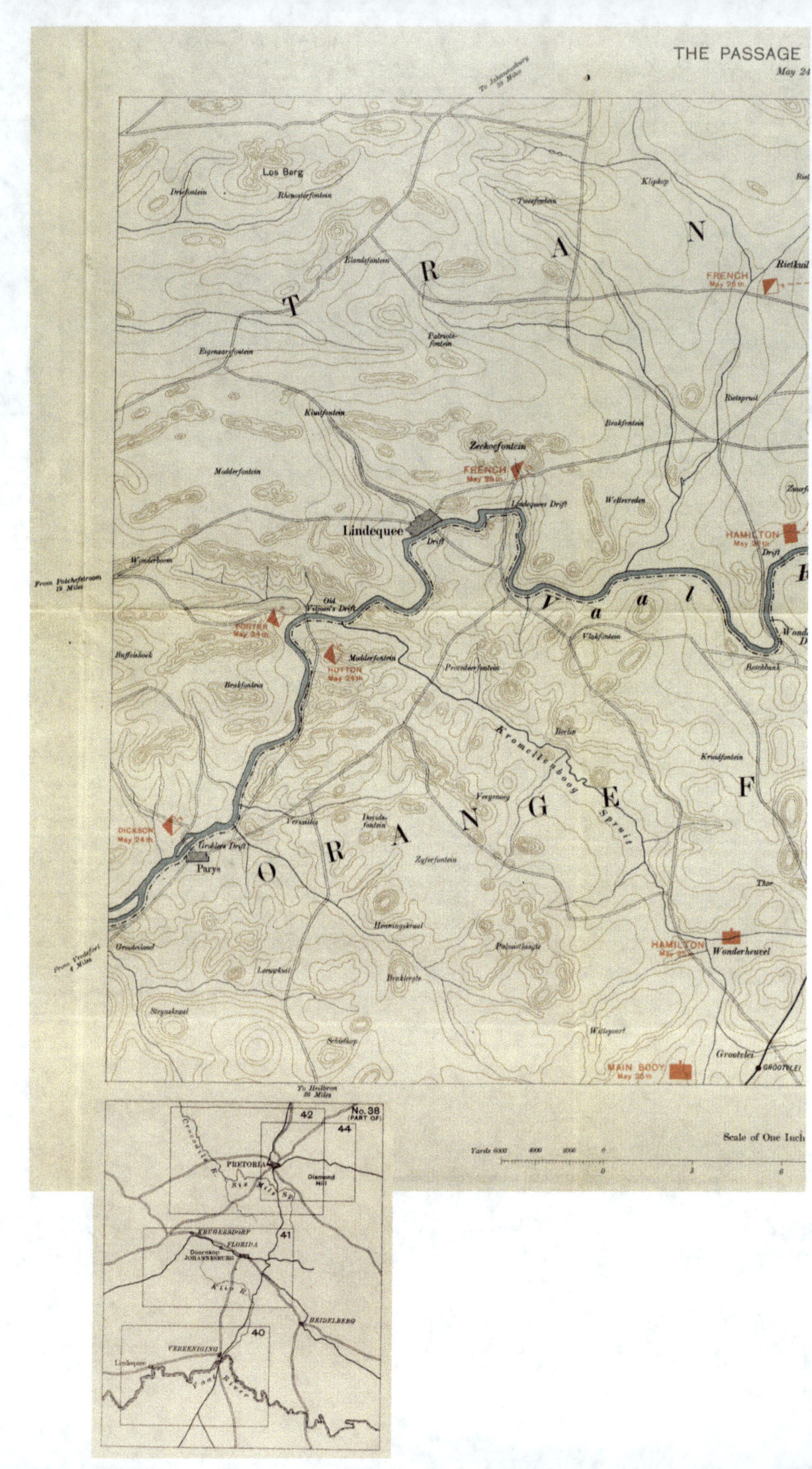

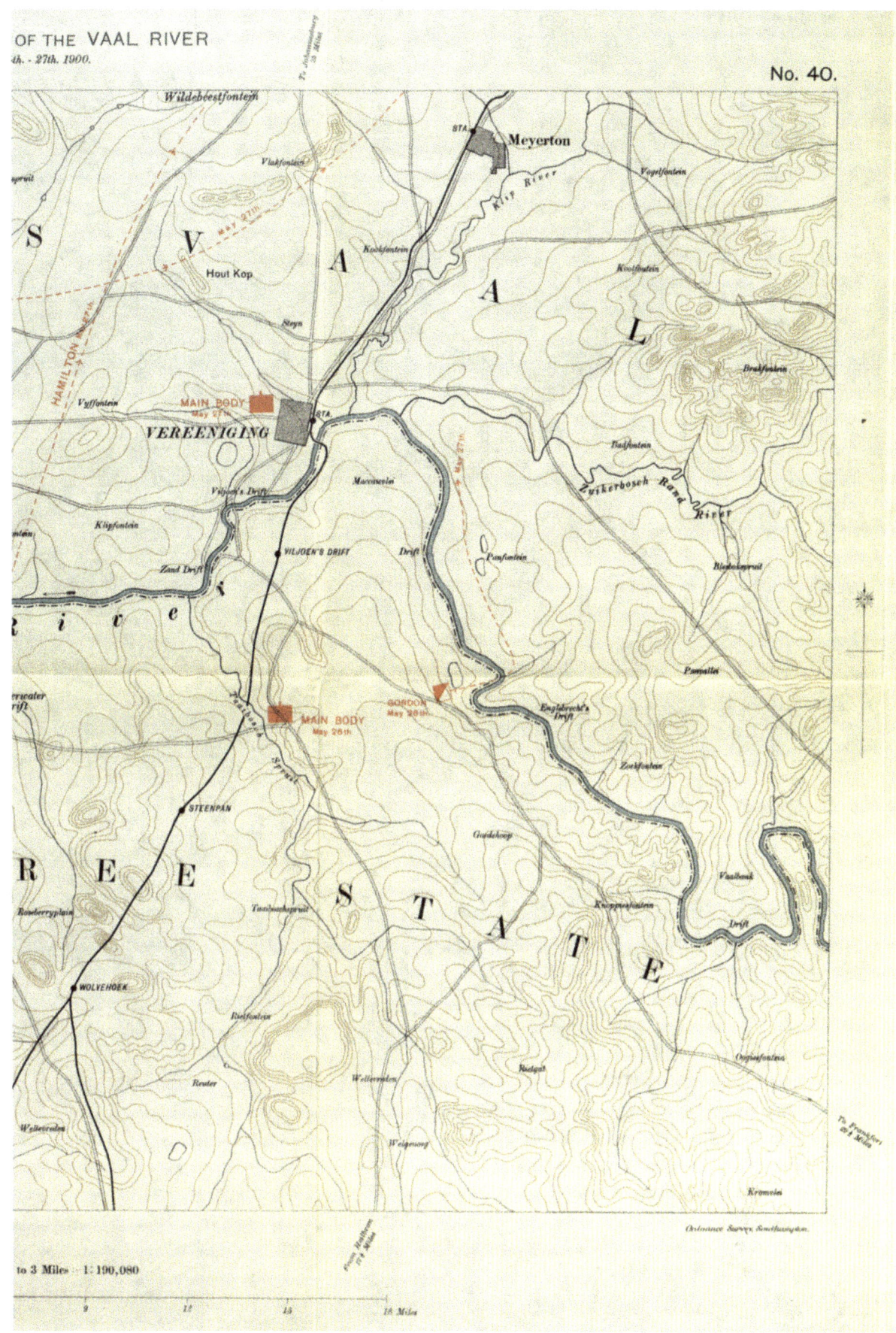

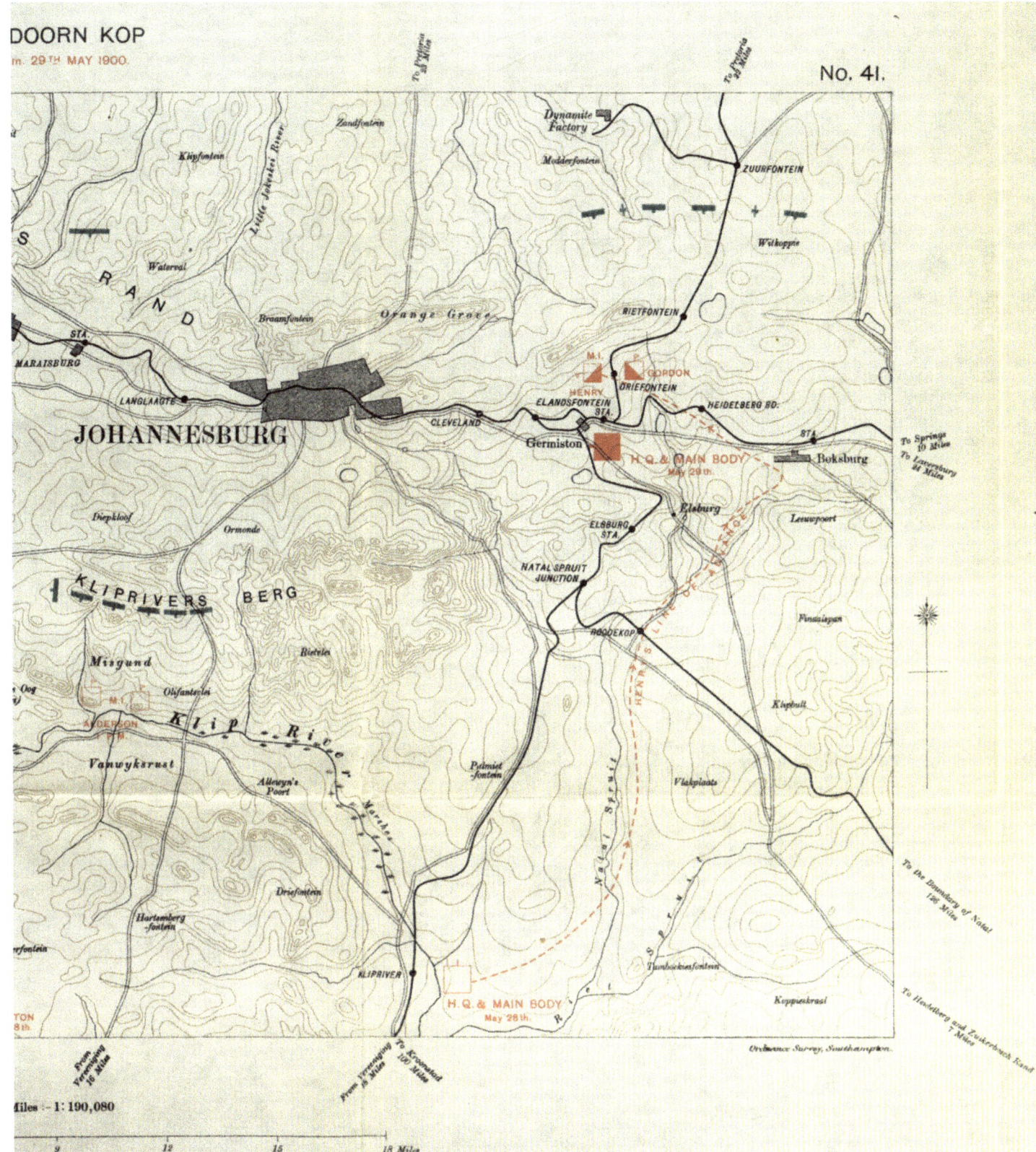

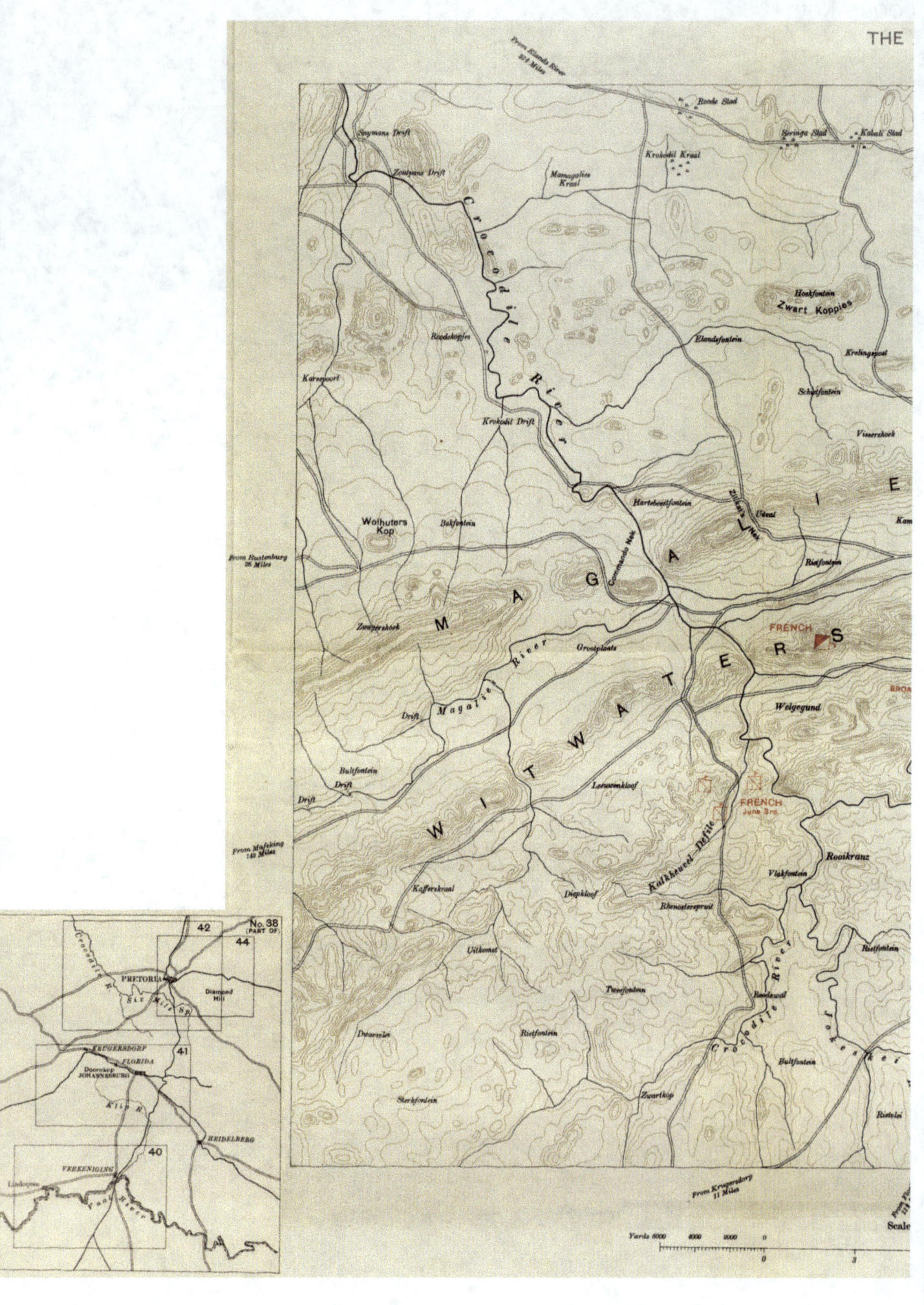

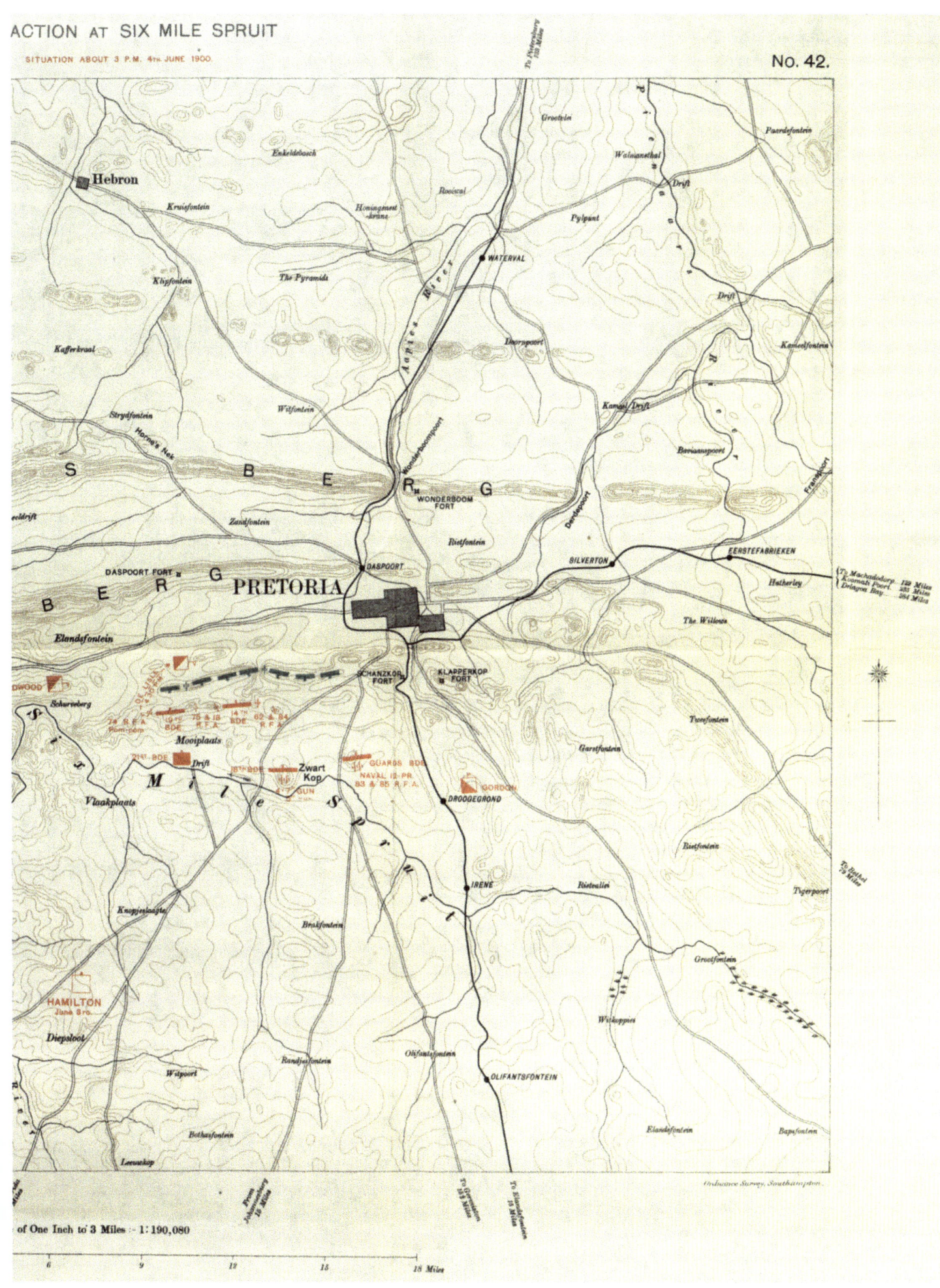

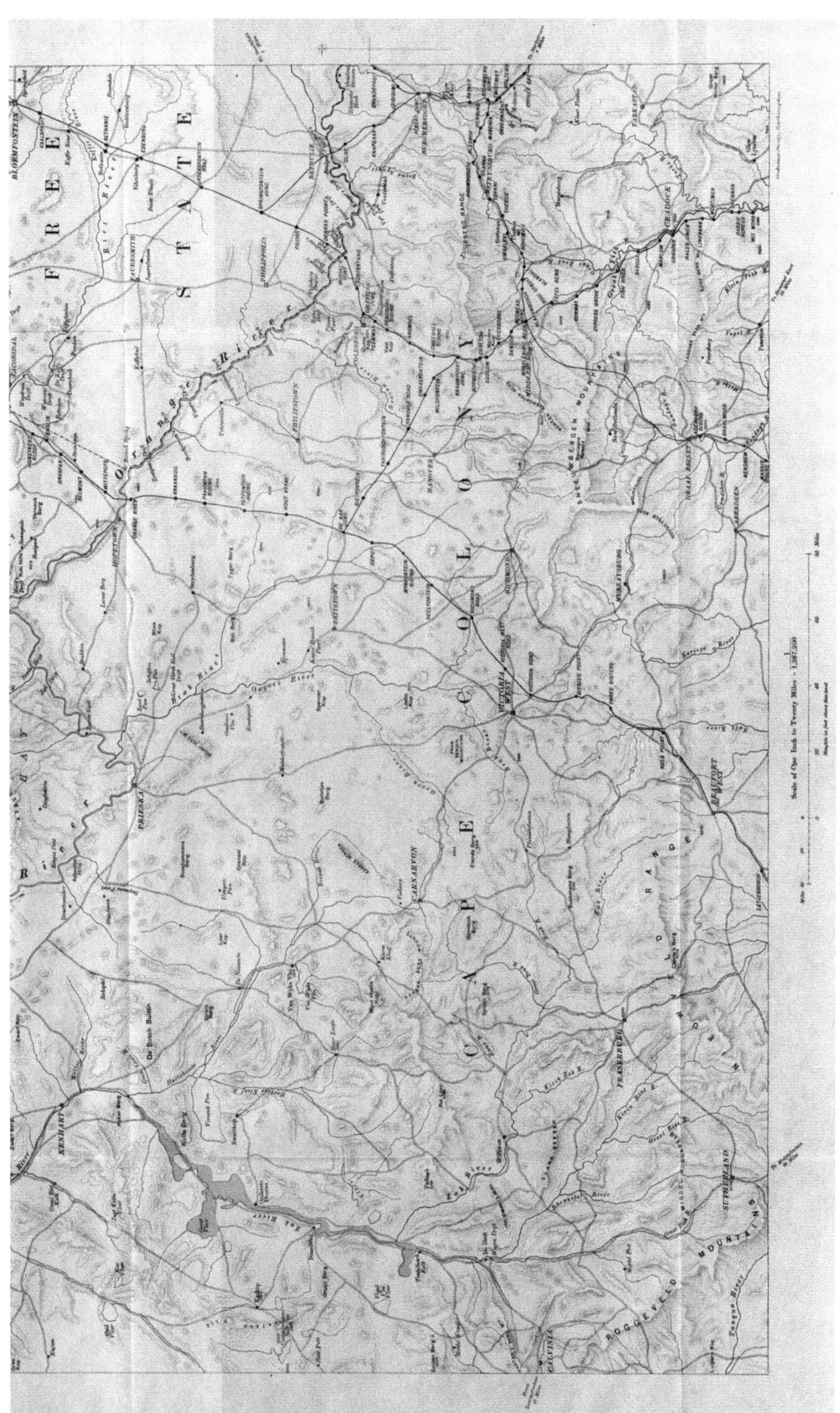

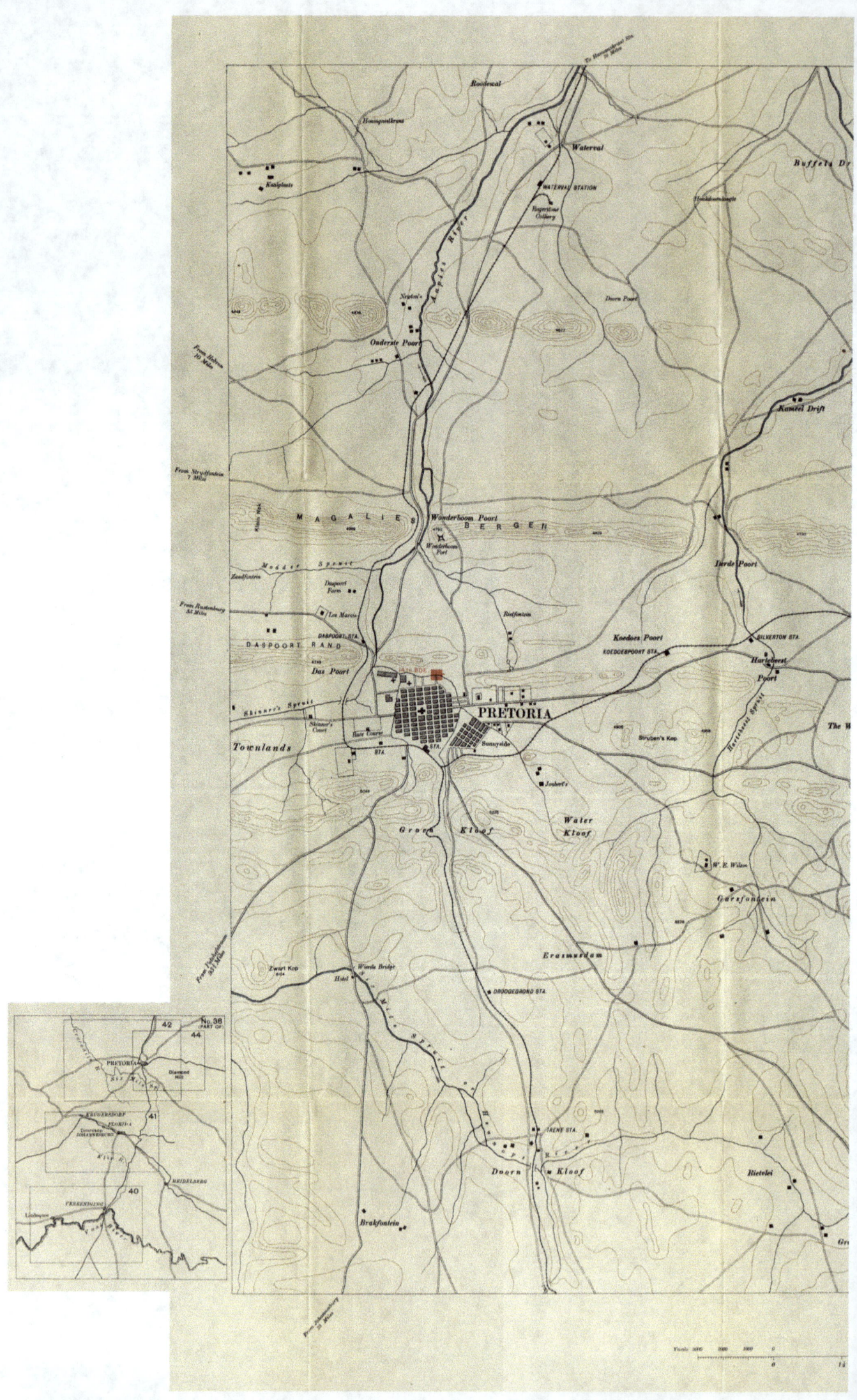

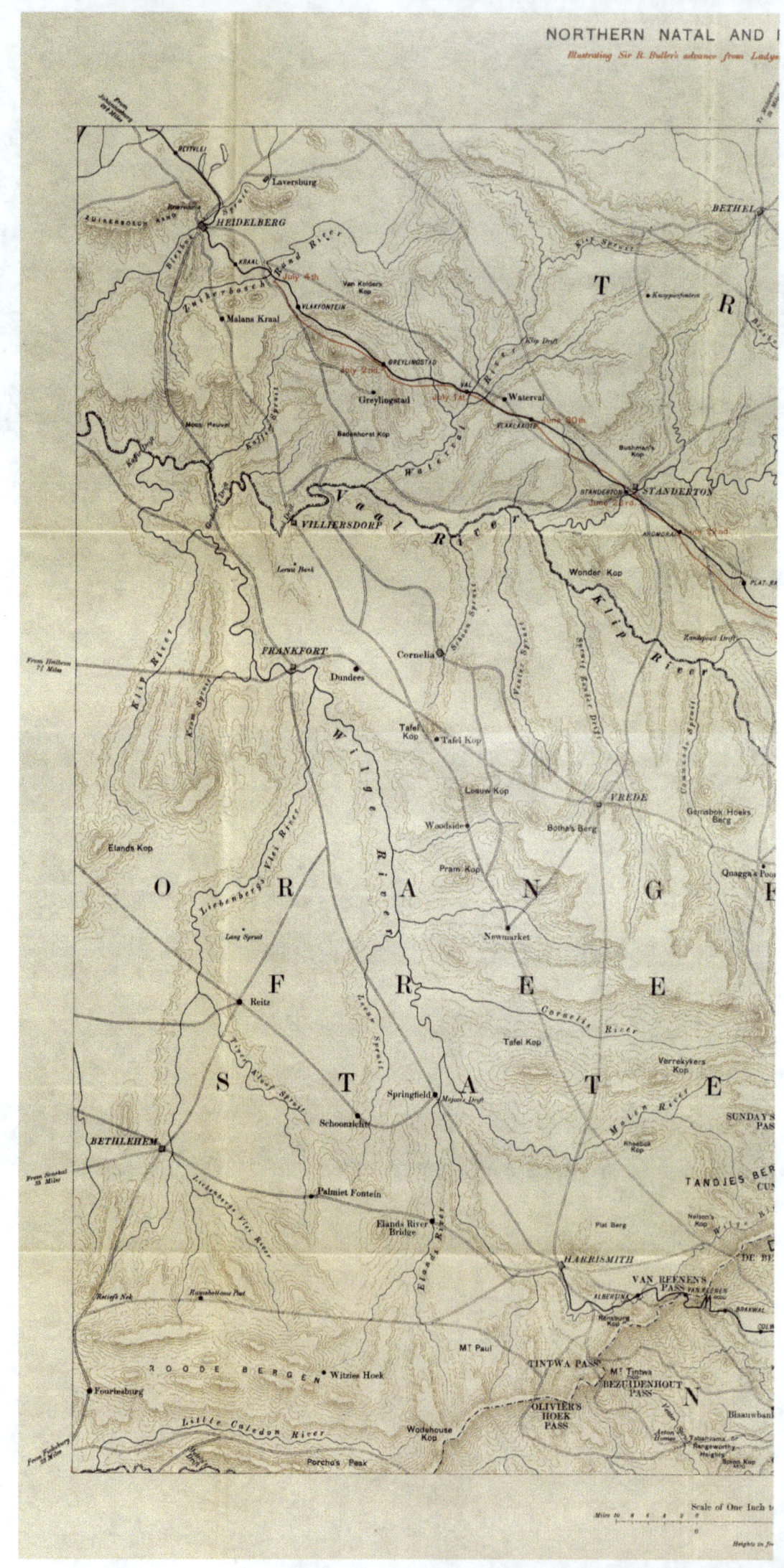

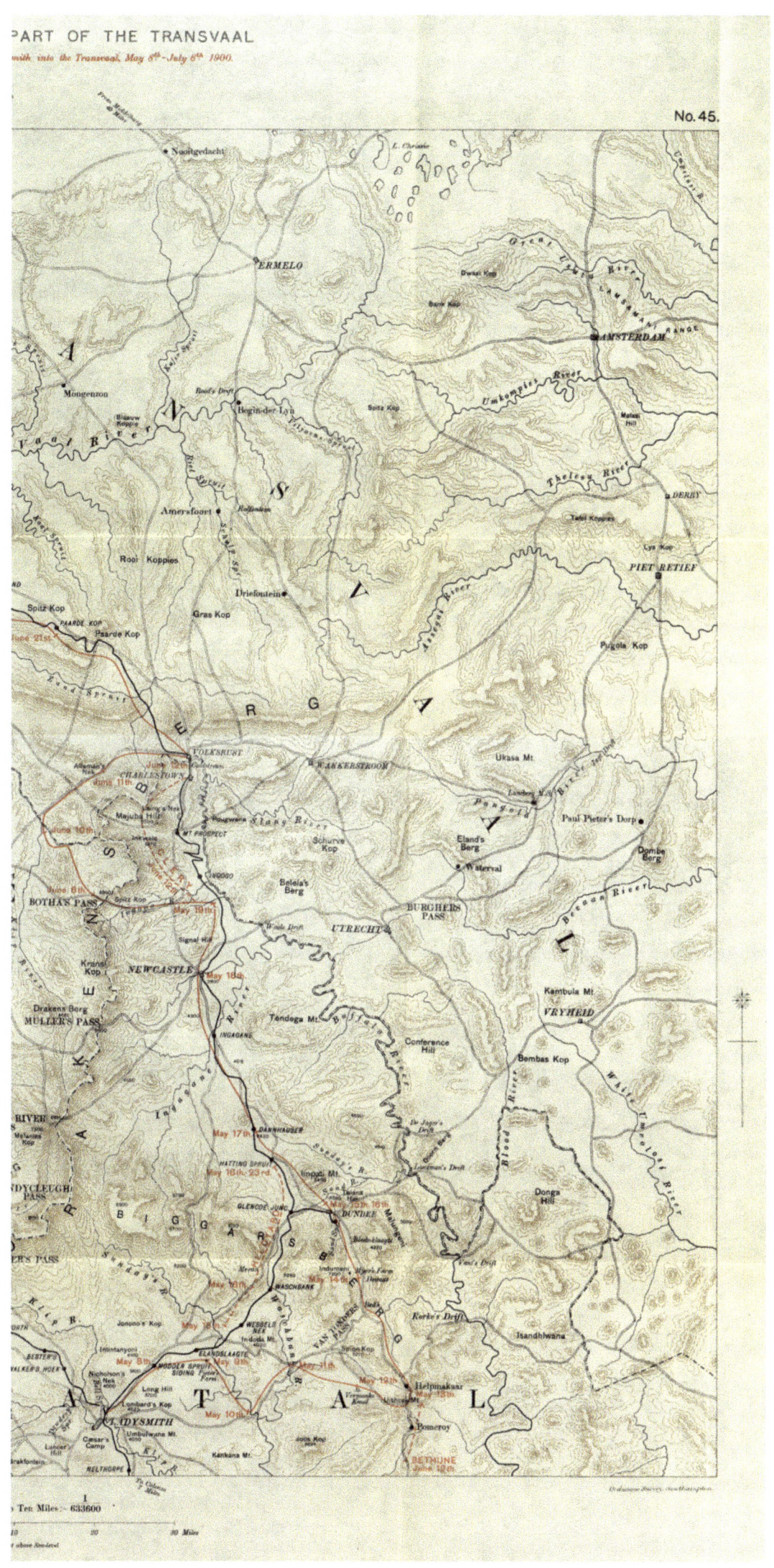

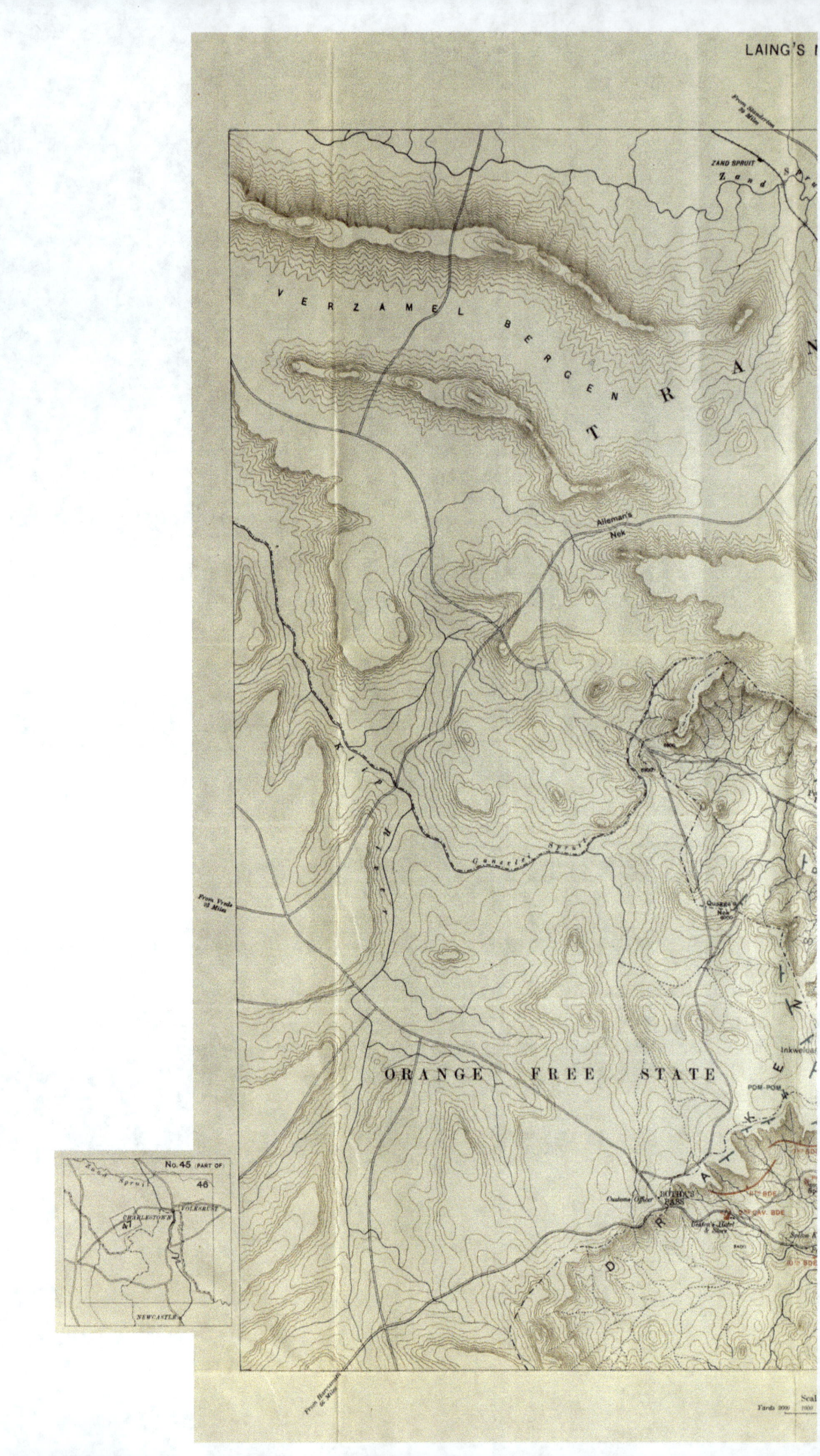

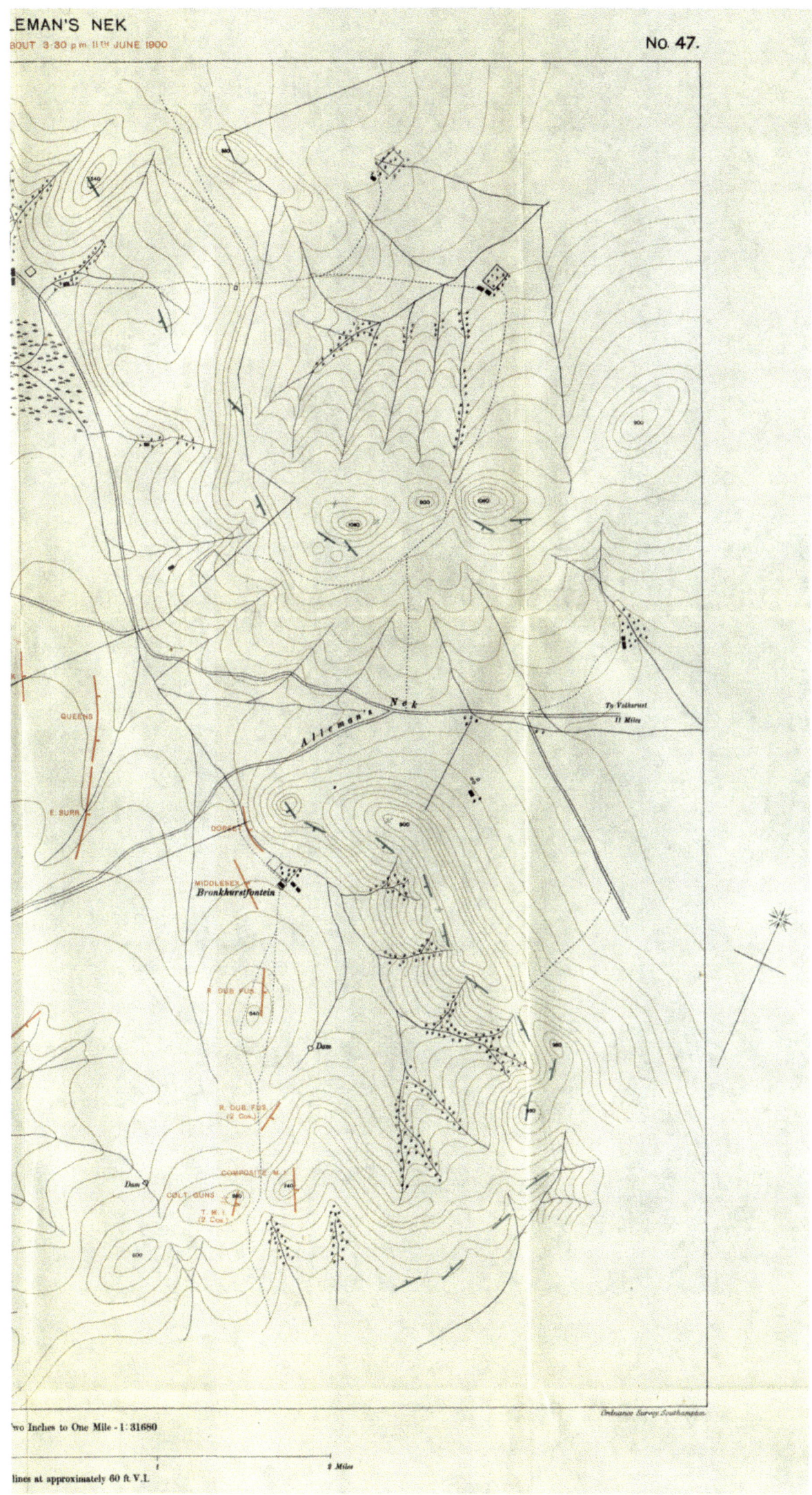

BELFAST TO KOOM

SHOWING THE SECOND STAGE OF THE COMBINED ADVANCE

Scale of One Inch to Six Miles

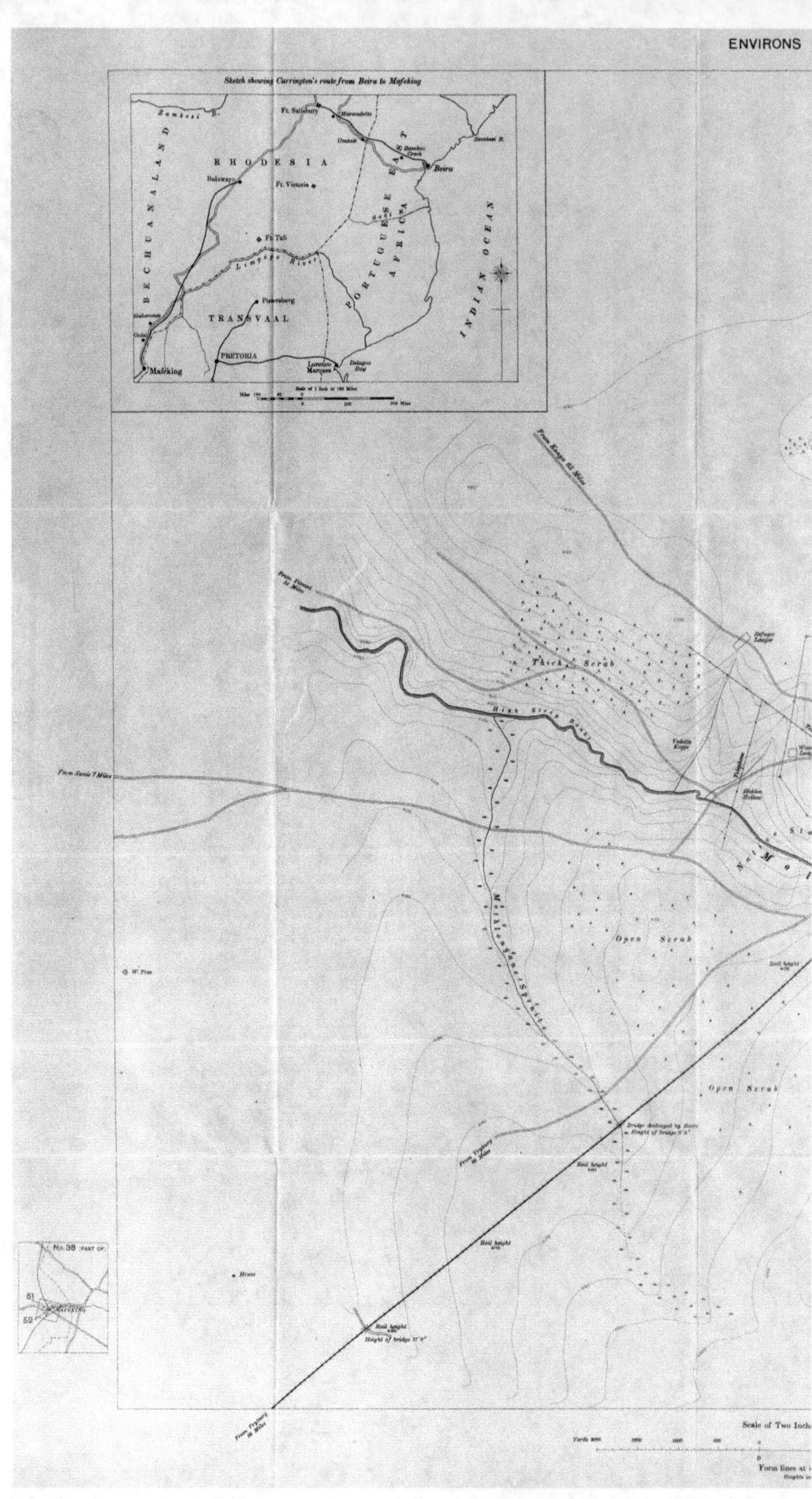

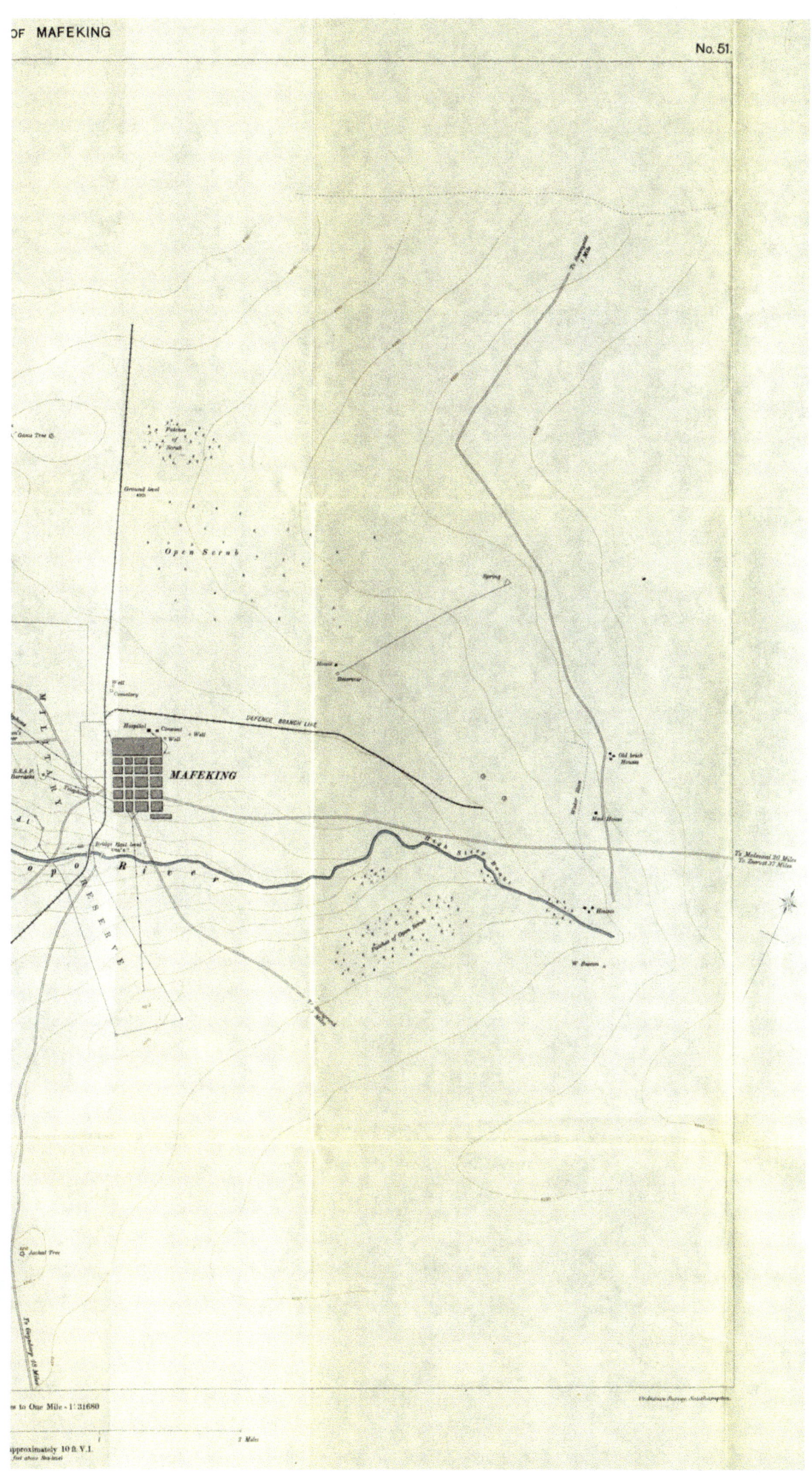

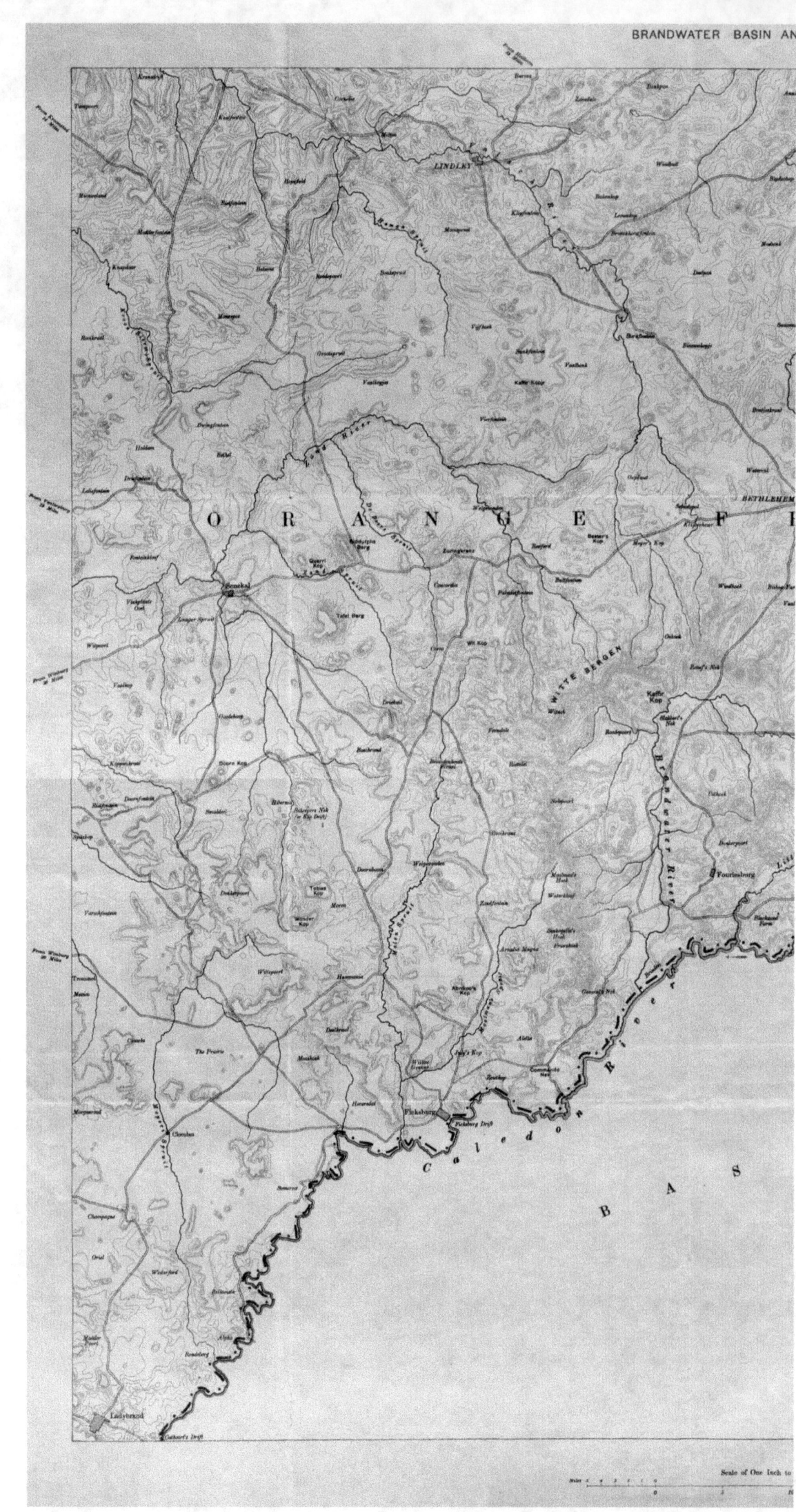

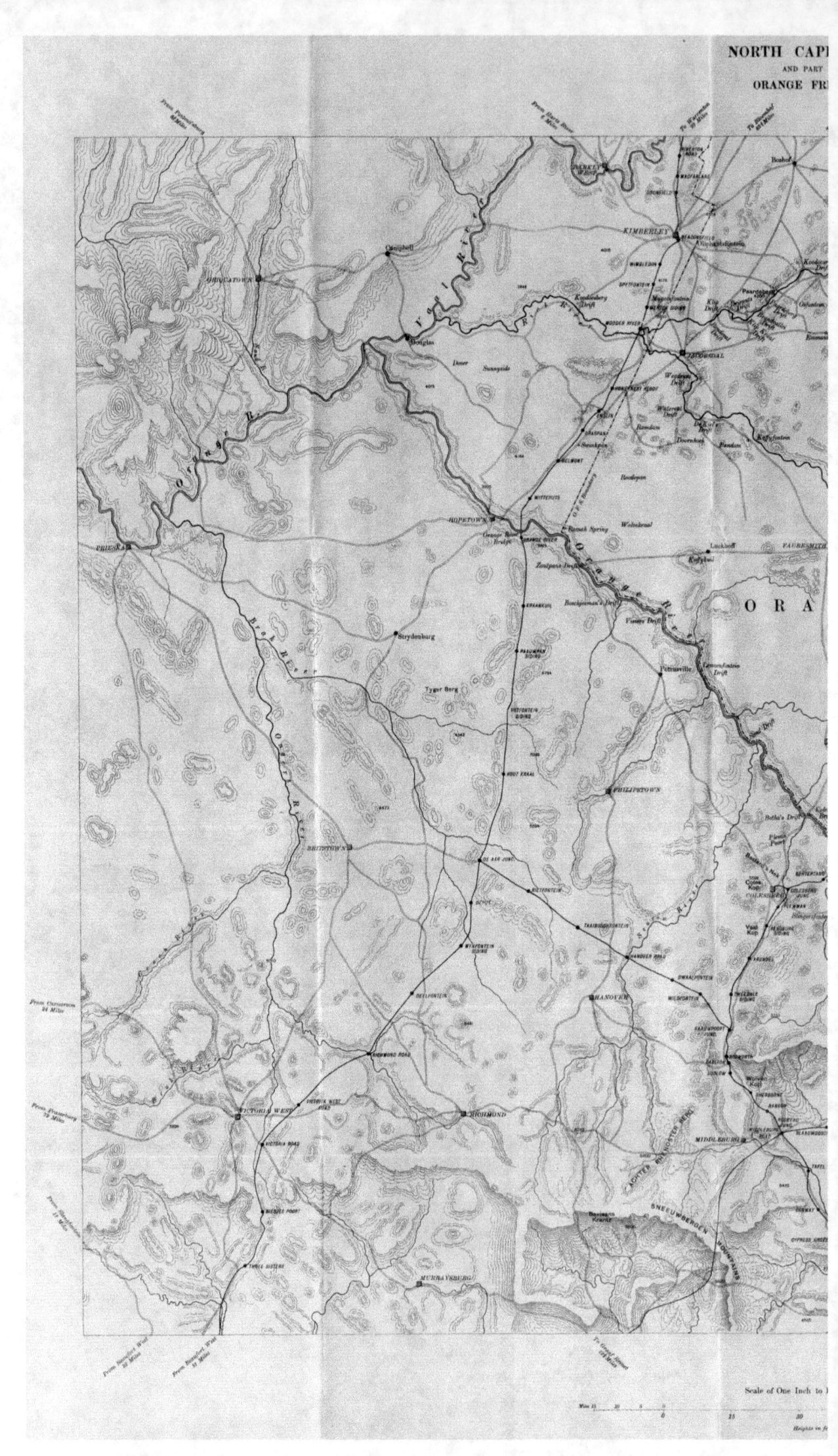

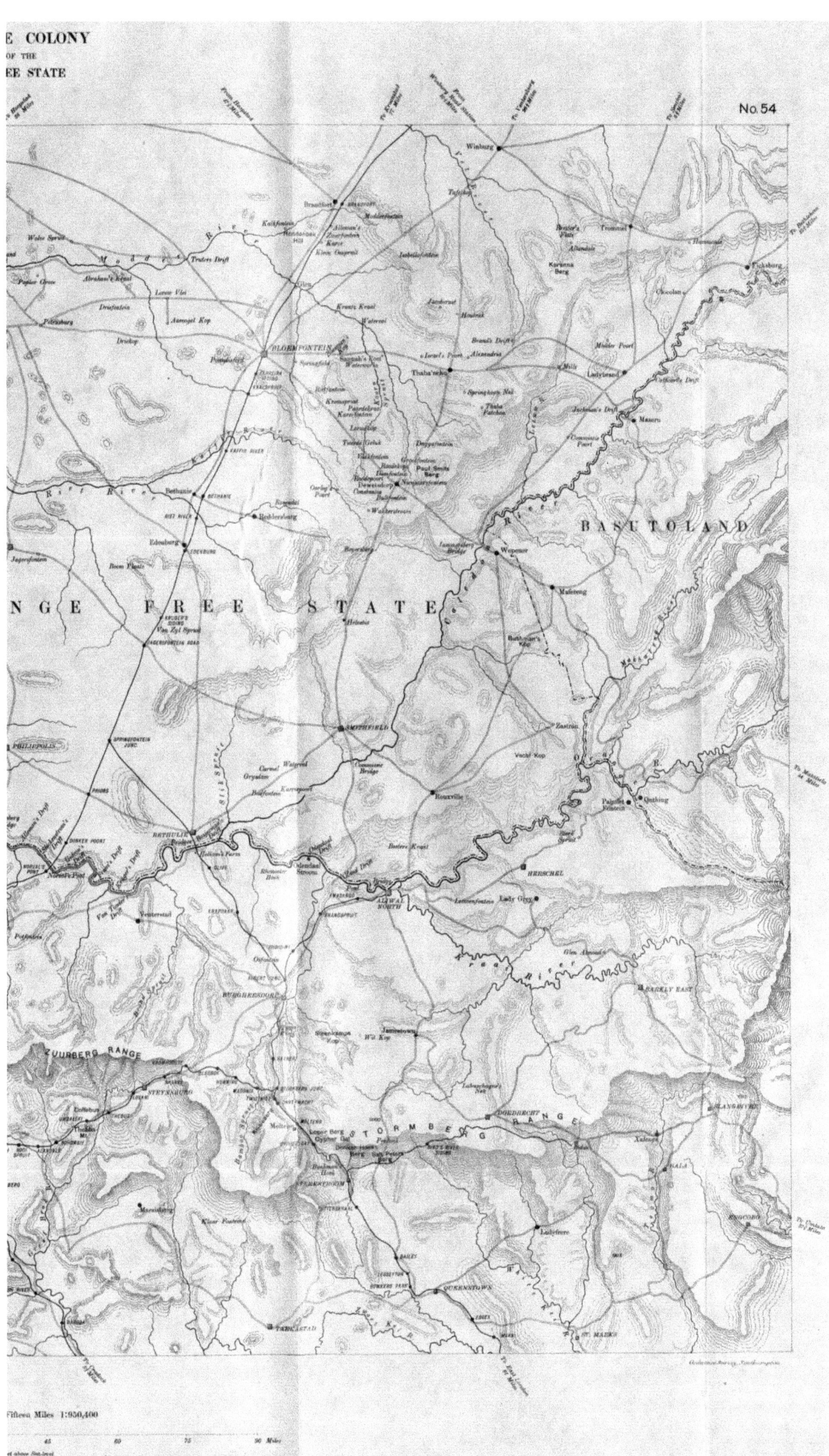

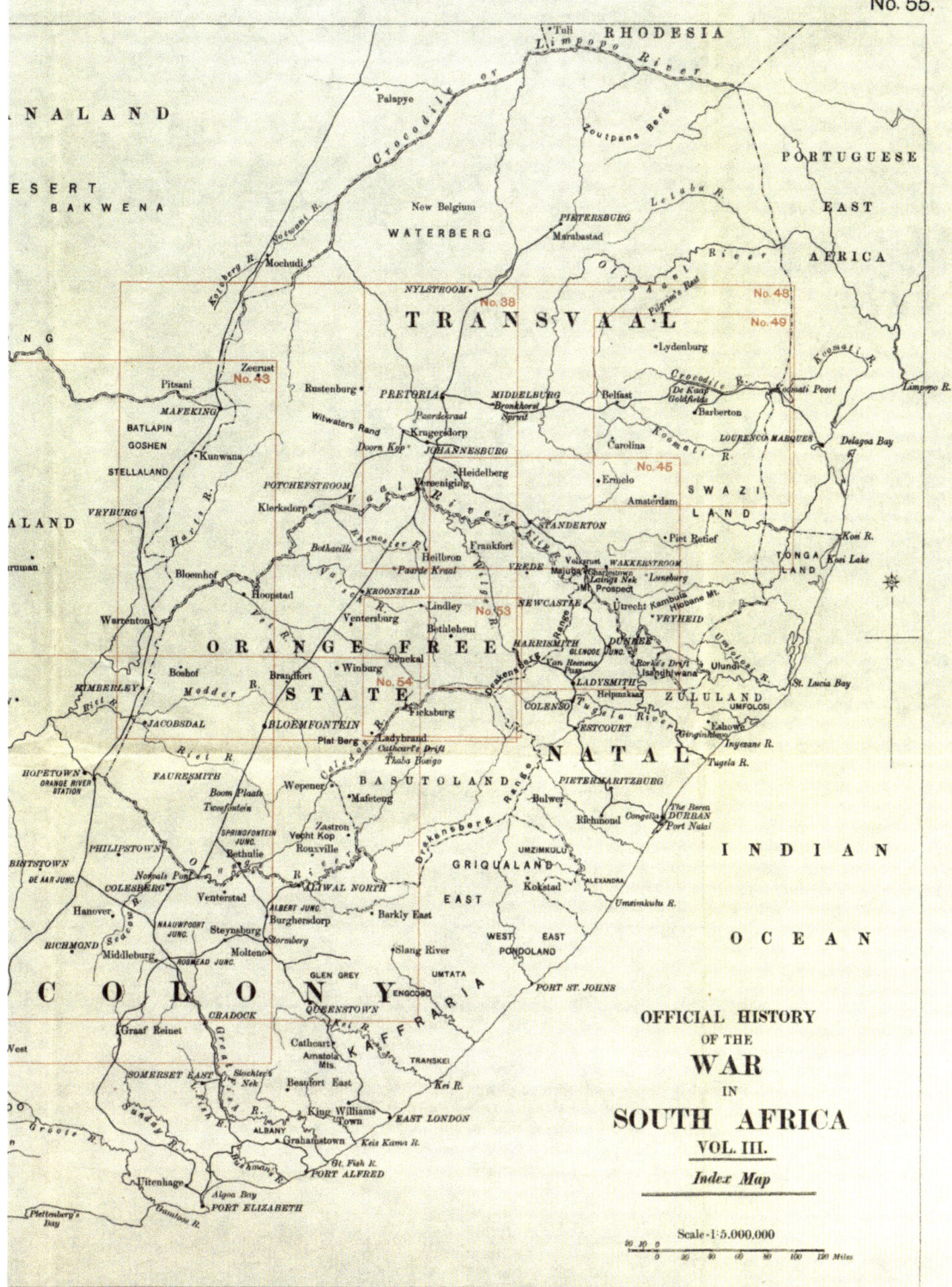

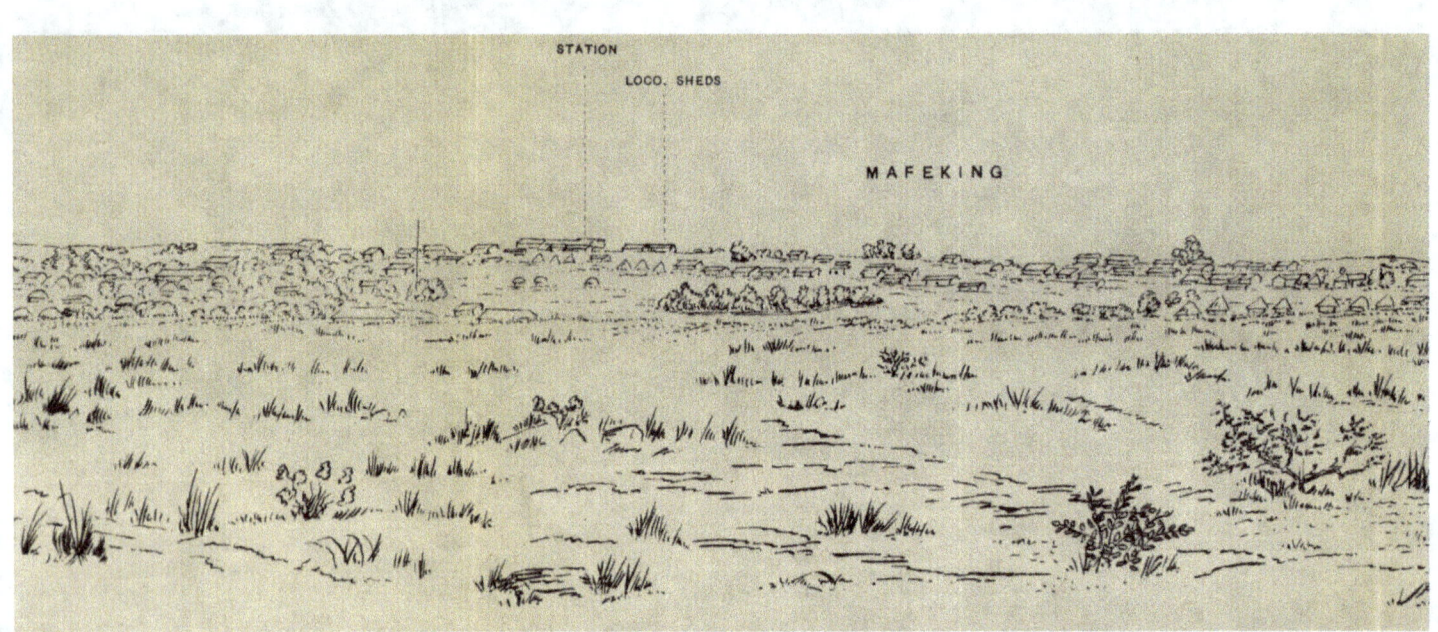

MAFEKING, AND SURROUNDING COUNTRY LOOKING NORTH FROM FORT MACKENZIE
FROM AN UNFINISHED SKETCH BY THE LATE CAPTAIN W.C.C.ERSKINE S.M.I.
COMPLETED BY MAJOR K.M.DAVIE GLOUCESTER REGIMENT

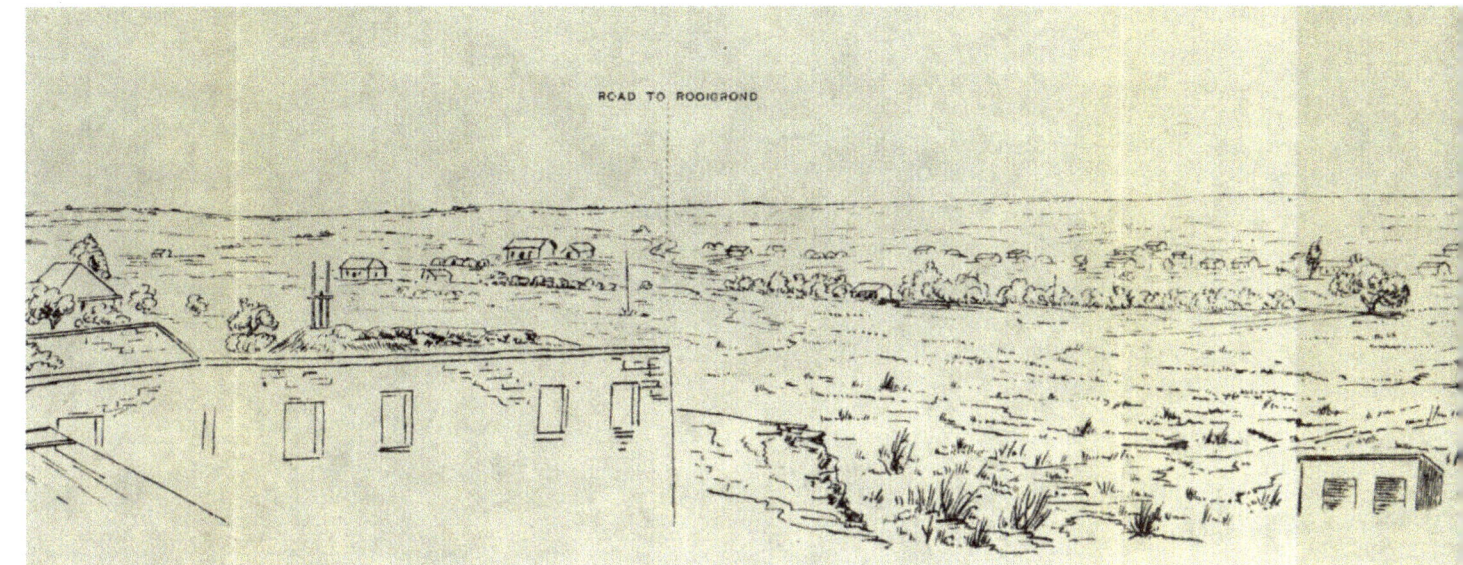

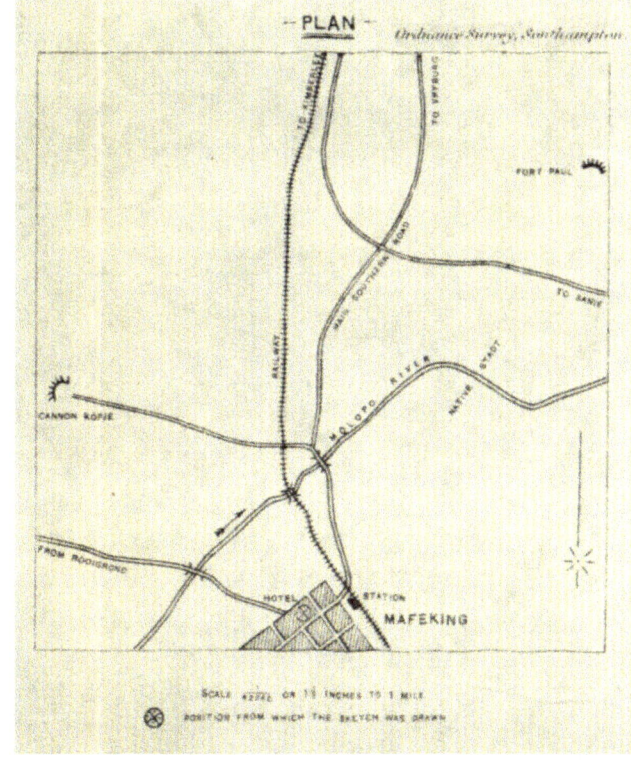

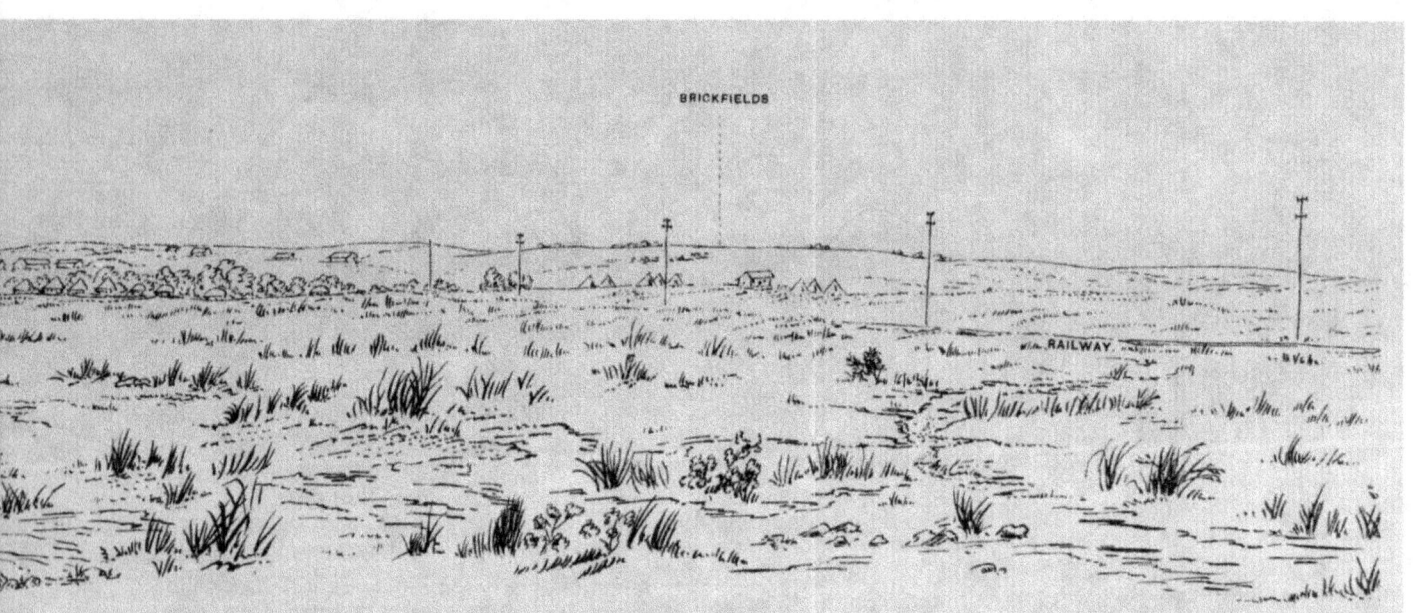

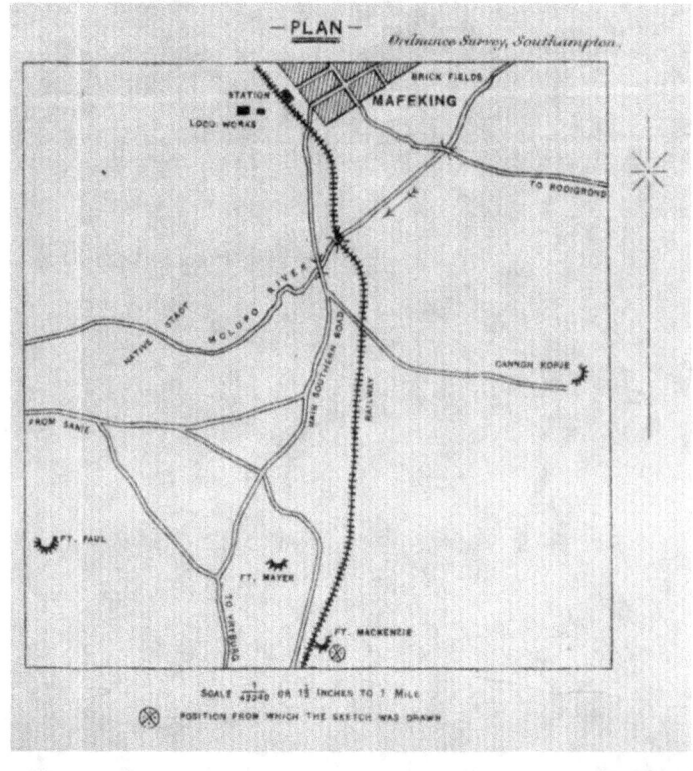

COUNTRY LOOKING SOUTH FROM MAFEKING
FROM AN UNFINISHED SKETCH BY THE LATE CAPTAIN W.C.C. ERSKINE B.M.I.
COMPLETED BY MAJOR K.M. DAVIE, GLOUCESTER REGIMENT

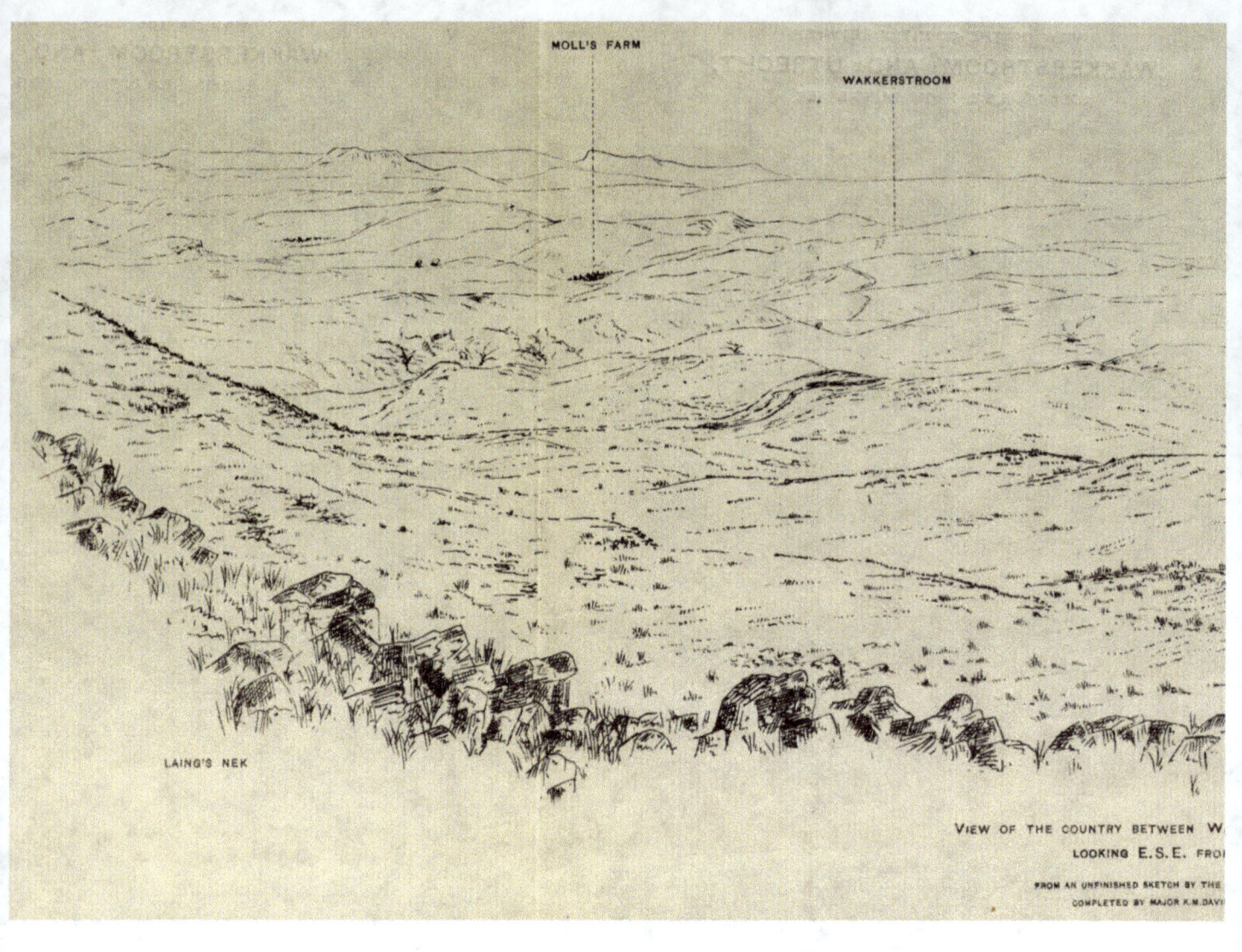

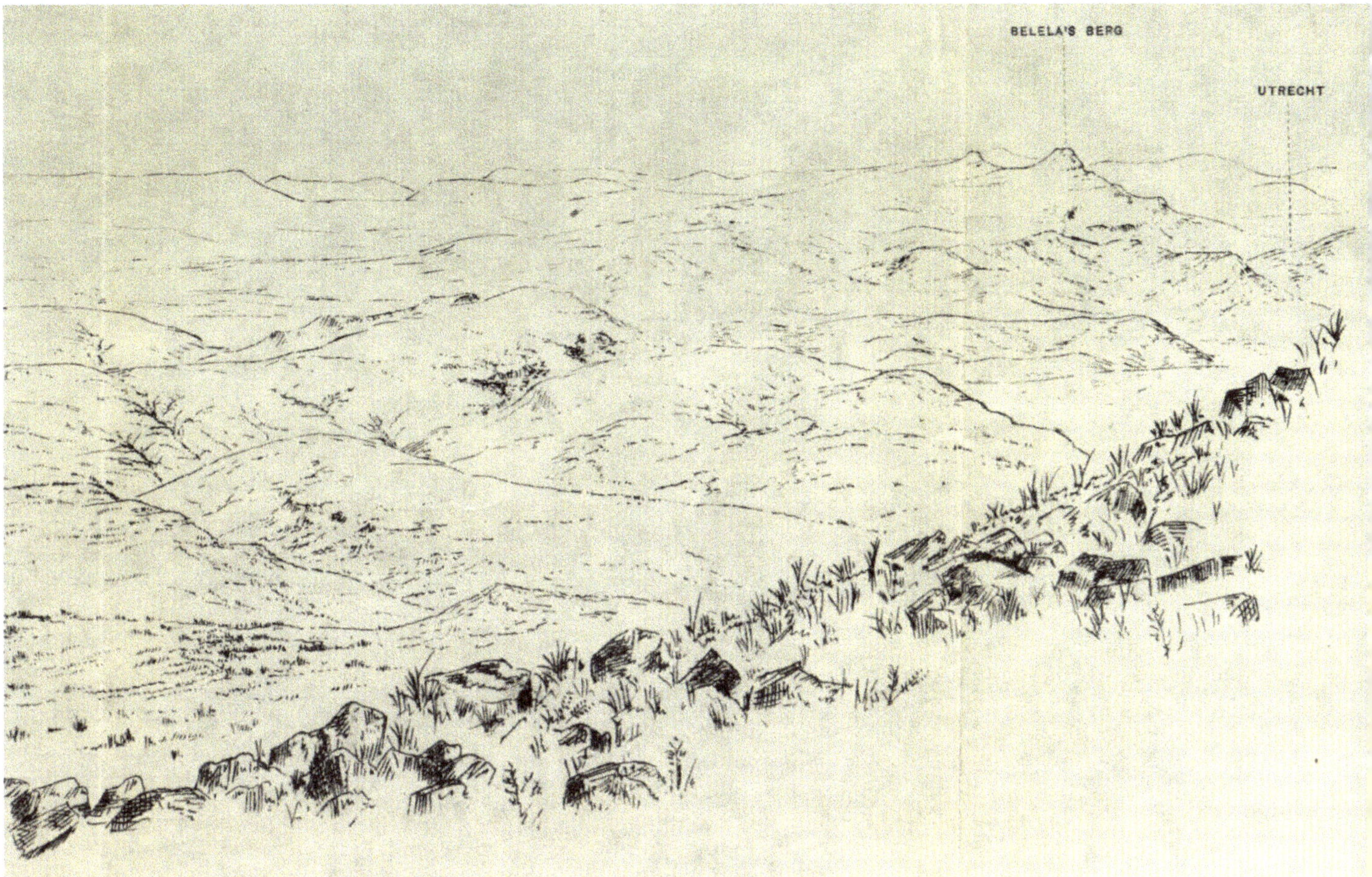

AKKERSTROOM AND UTRECHT,
M LAING'S NEK
LATE CAPTAIN W.C.C. ERSKINE, B.M.I.
E GLOUCESTER REGIMENT

Ordnance Survey, Southampton.

—PLAN—

SCALE $\frac{1}{506880}$ OR 1 INCH TO 8 MILES

⊗ POSITION FROM WHICH THE SKETCH WAS DRAWN

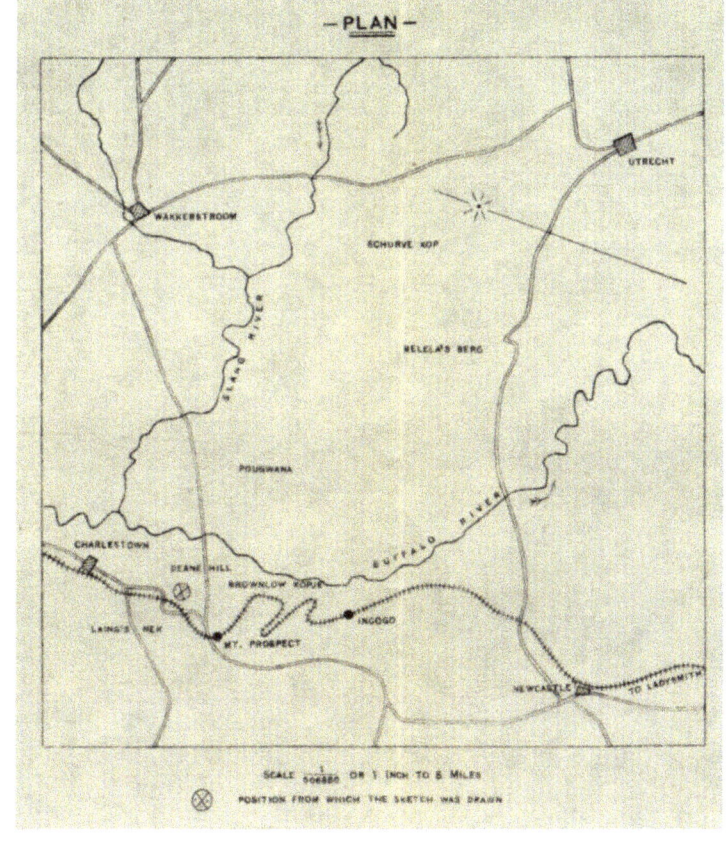

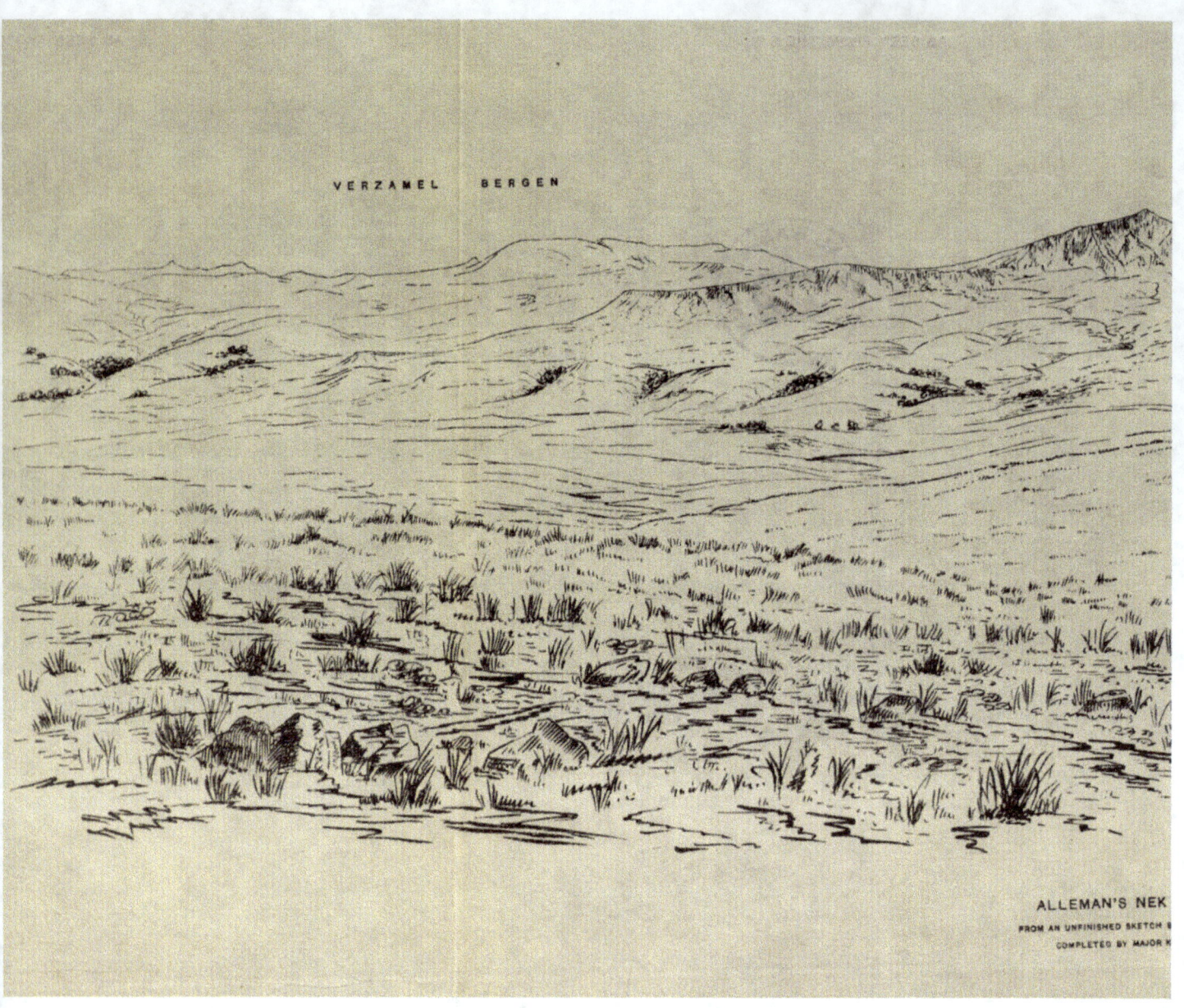

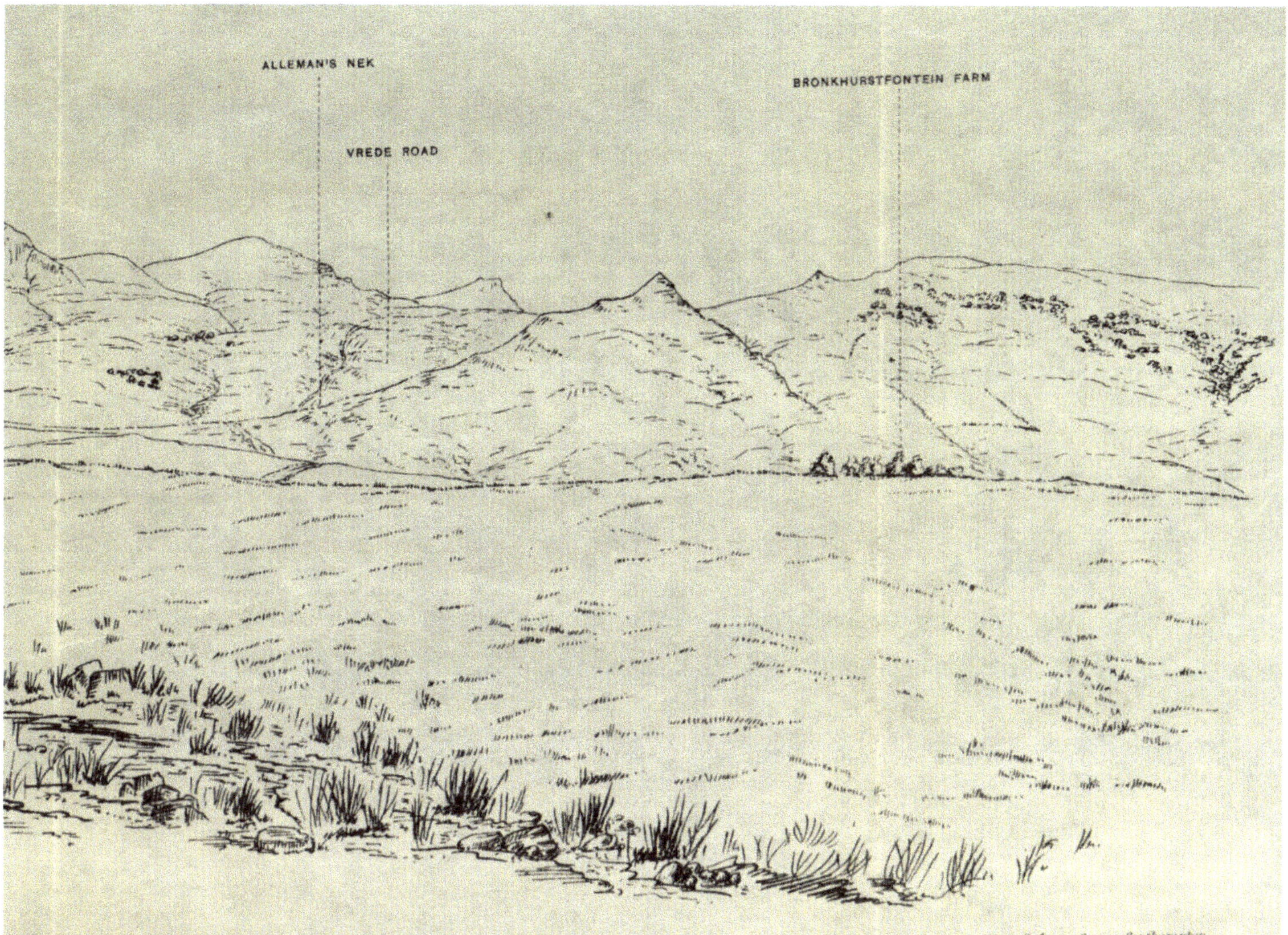

ALLEMAN'S NEK
VREDE ROAD
BRONKHURSTFONTEIN FARM

Ordnance Survey, Southampton.

AS SEEN FROM THE S.W.

Y THE LATE CAPTAIN W.C.C.ERSKINE, B.M.I.

.M.DAVIE GLOUCESTER REGIMENT

– PLAN –

1080
900
1080
TO VOLKSRUST 12 MILES
ALLEMAN'S NEK
900
BRONKHURSTFONTEIN FARM
FROM VREDE 30 MILES

SCALE $\frac{1}{63360}$ OR 1 INCH TO 1 MILE

POSITION FROM WHICH THE SKETCH WAS DRAWN

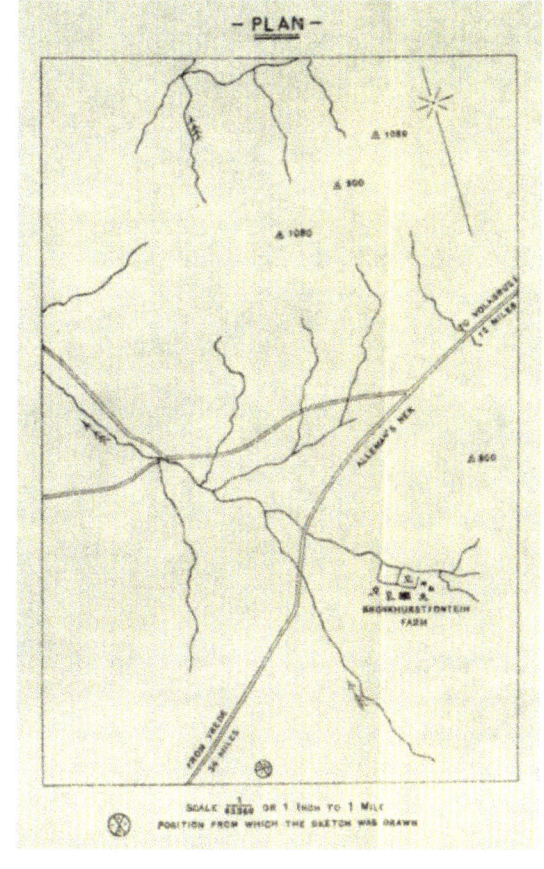

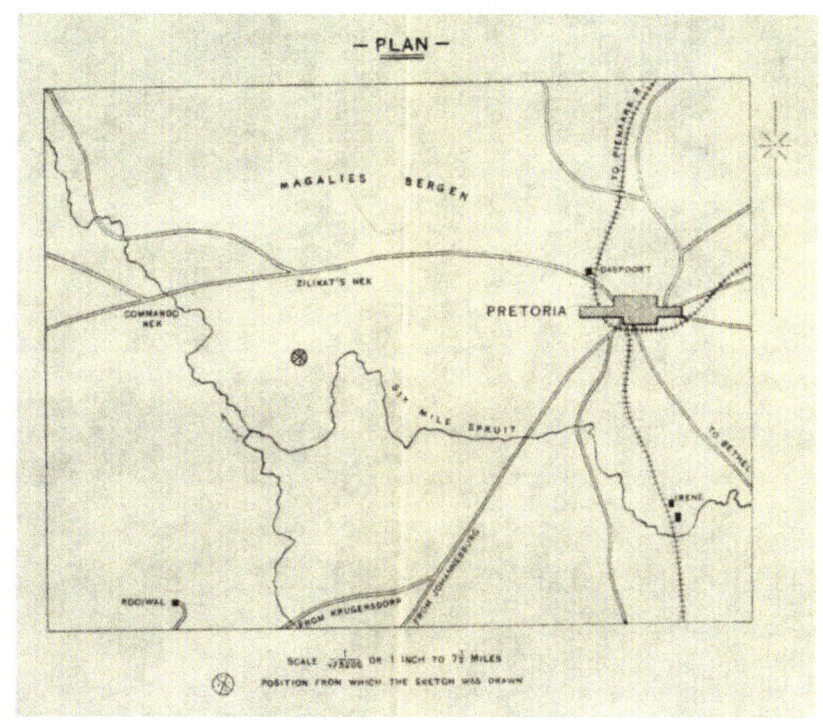

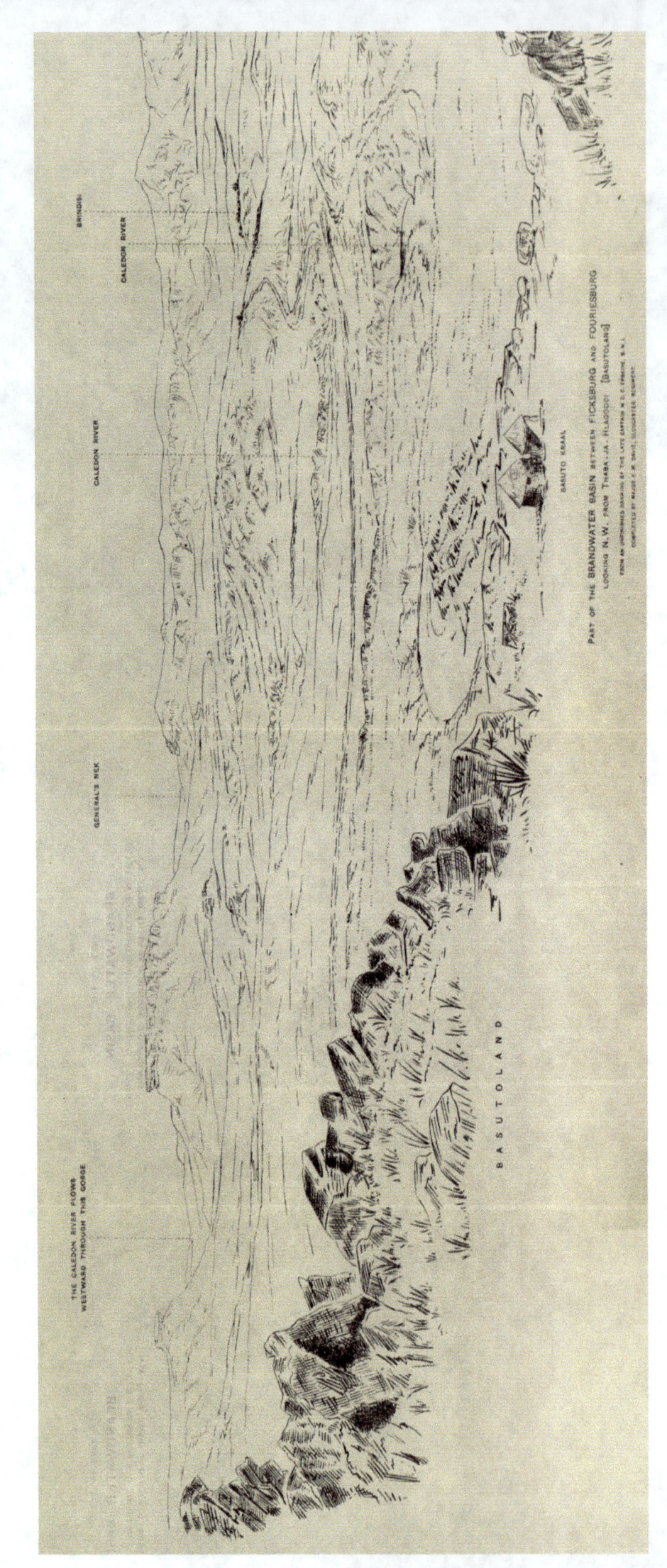

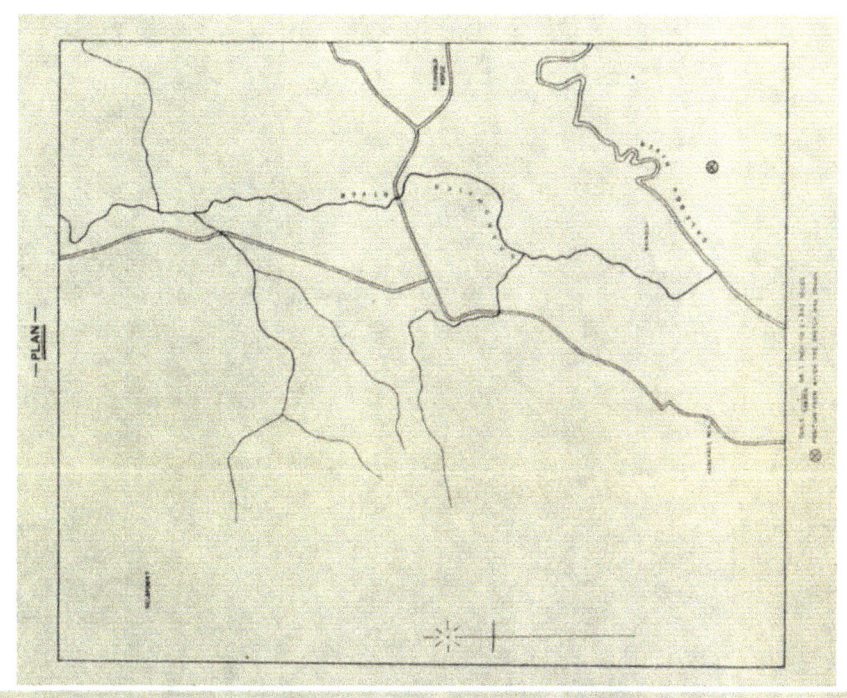

RETIEF'S NEK, LOOKING S.W., FROM OUTSIDE THE BRANDWATER BASIN.

FROM AN UNFINISHED DRAWING BY THE LATE CAPTAIN W.O.C. ERSKINE, S.M.I.
COMPLETED BY MAJOR K. M. DAVIE, GLOUCESTER REGIMENT.

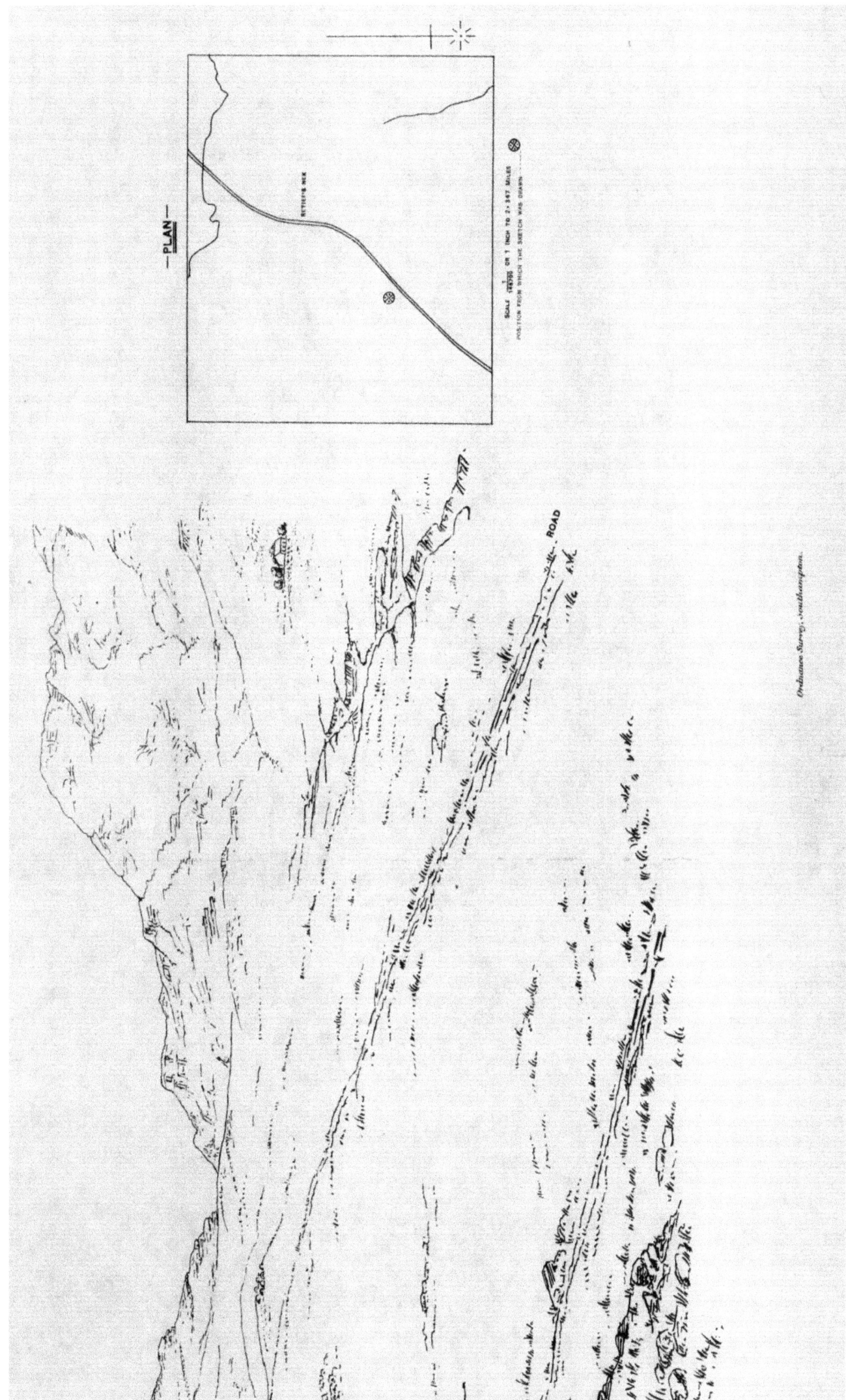

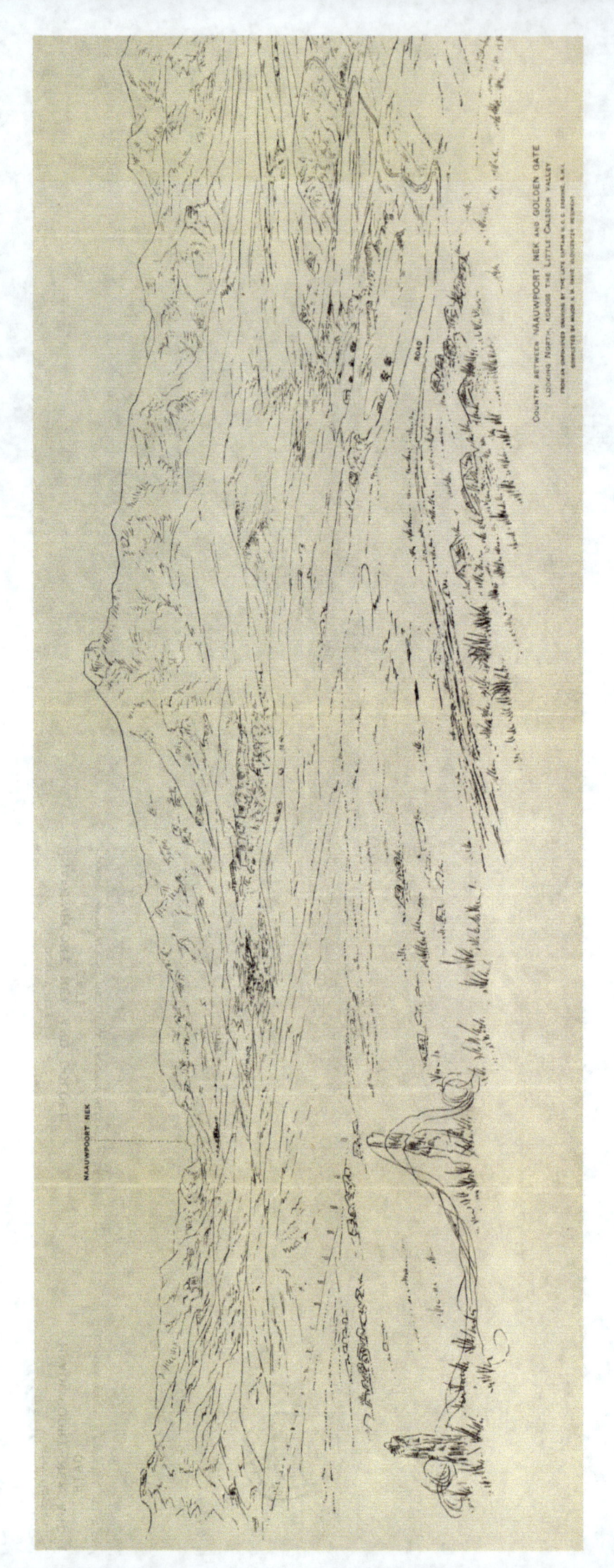

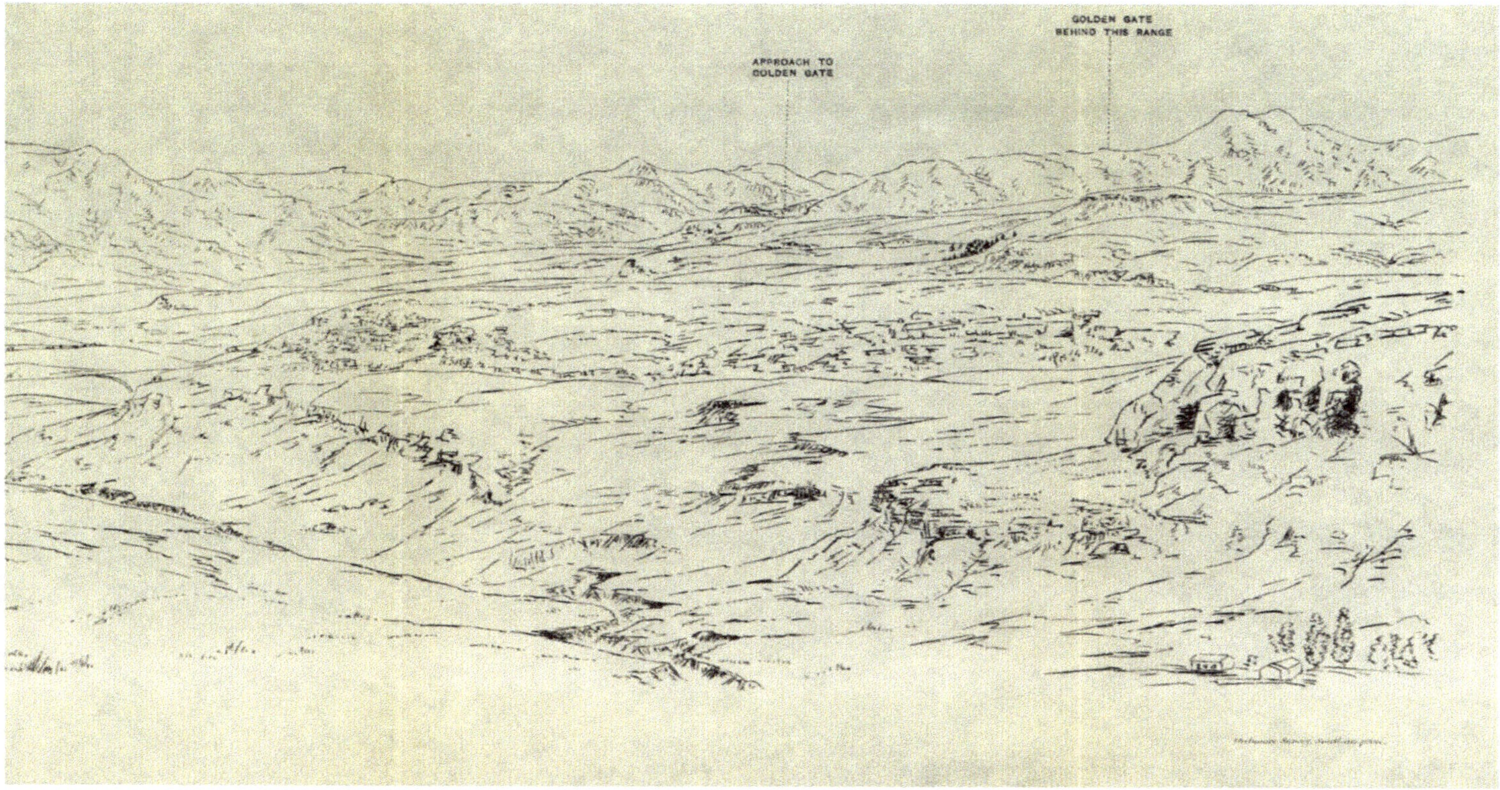
APPROACH TO
GOLDEN GATE
GOLDEN GATE
BEHIND THIS RANGE

PLAN
LITTLE CALEDON RIVER
GOLDEN GATE

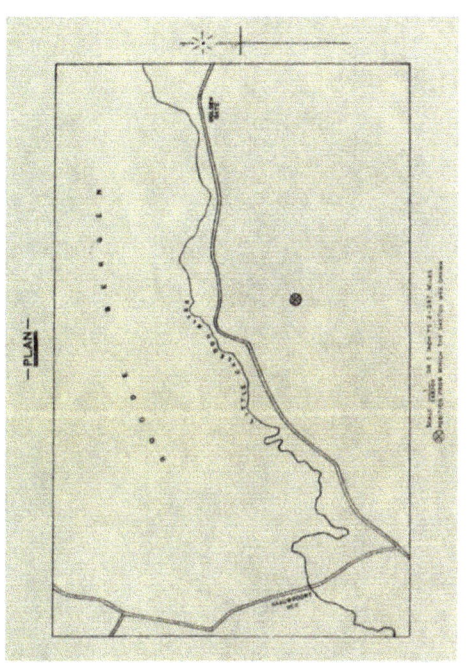

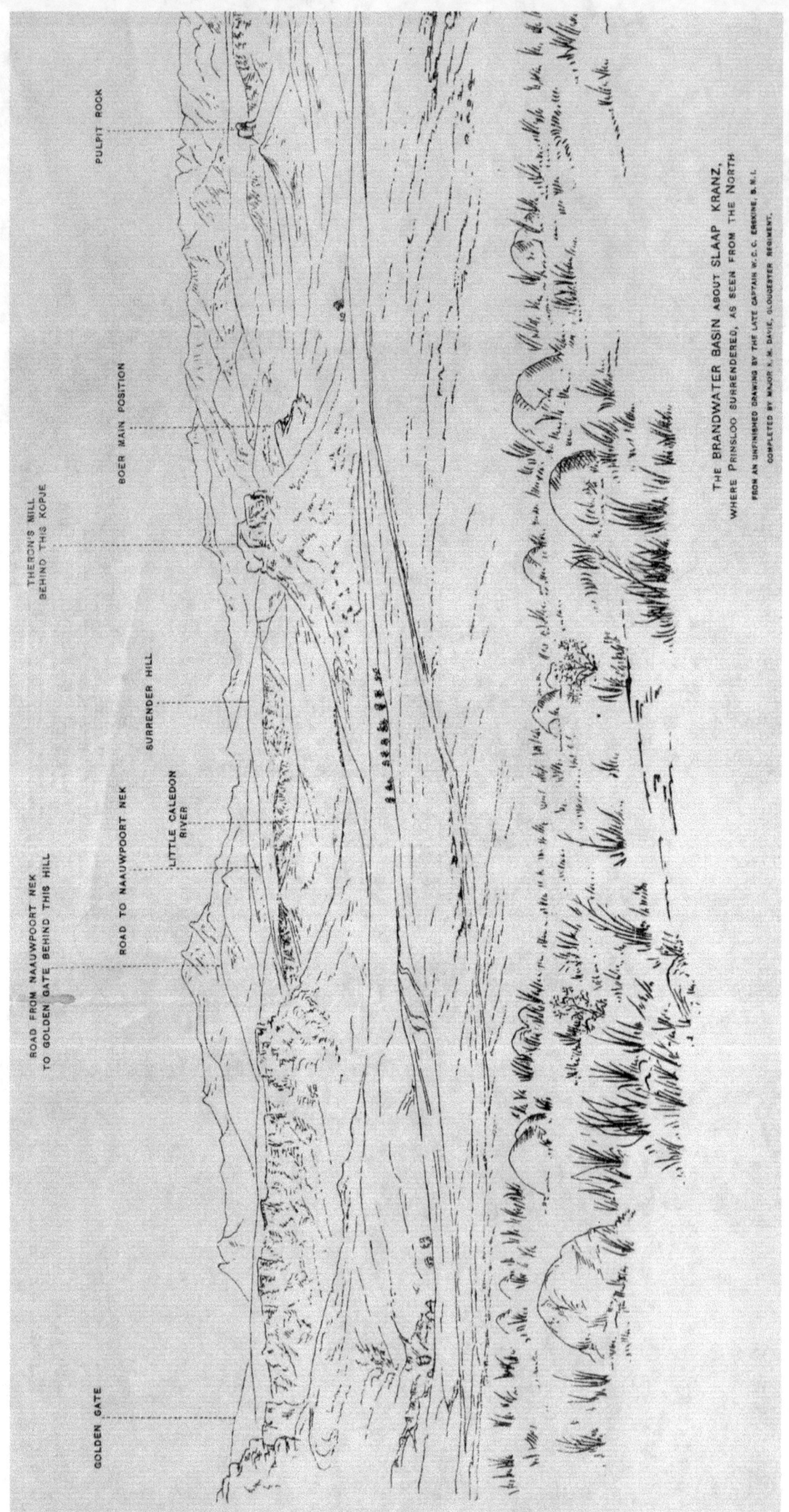

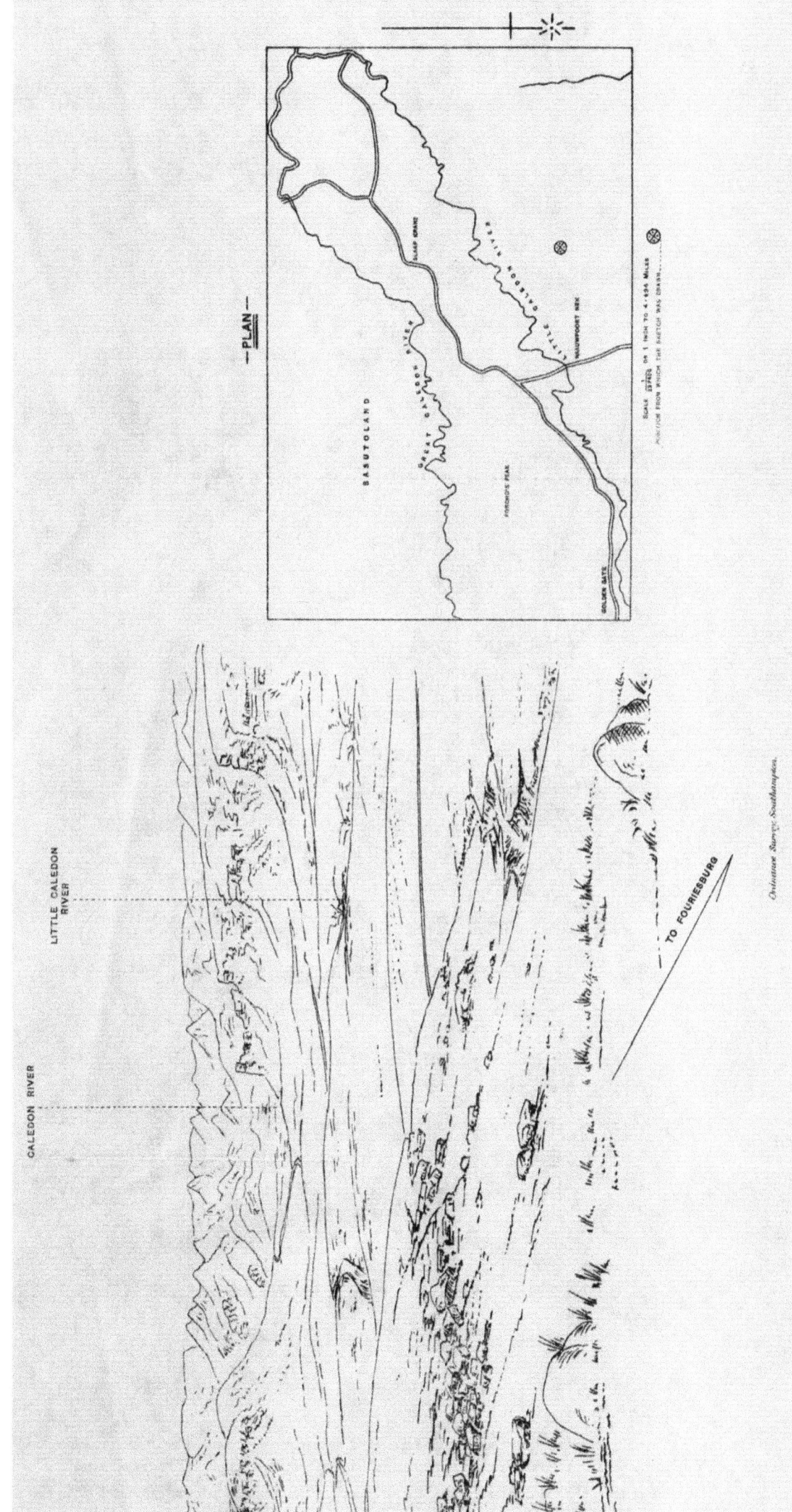

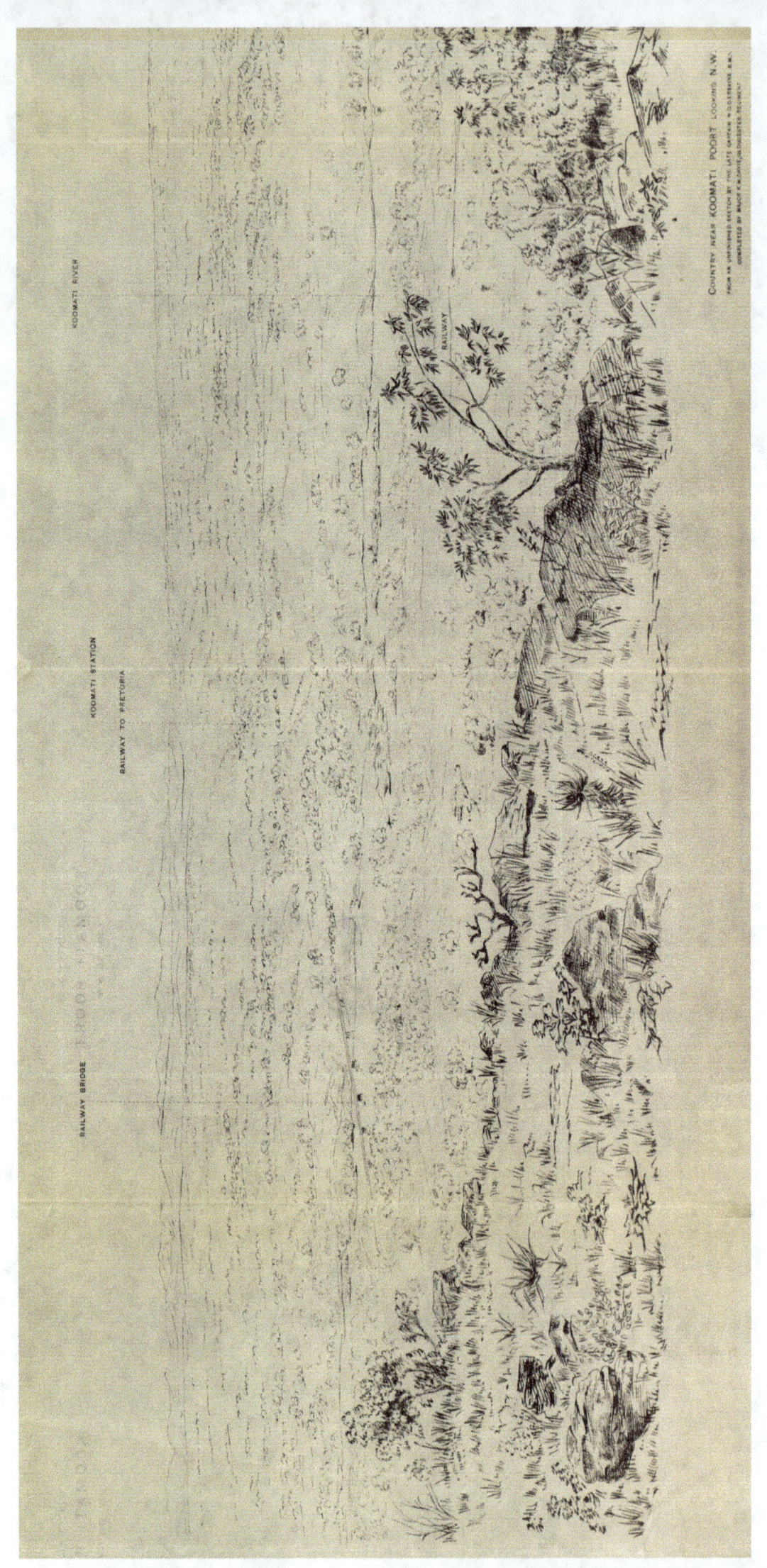

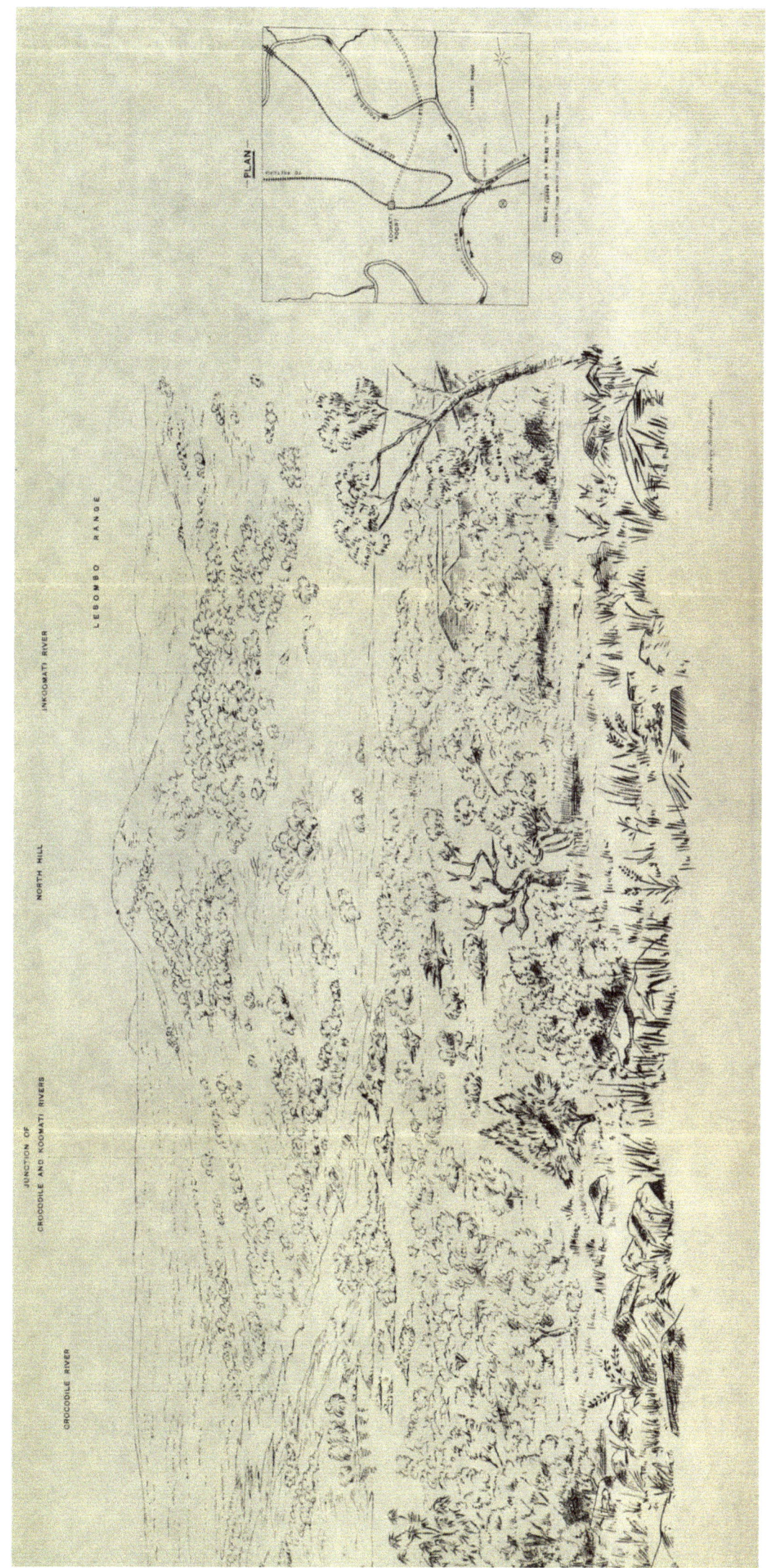